Spirit Guides and Archangels

The Communication Guide to Connecting with Spirits

© Copyright 2023 - All rights reserved.

The content contained within this book may not be reproduced, duplicated, or transmitted without direct written permission from the author or the publisher.

Under no circumstances will any blame or legal responsibility be held against the publisher, or author, for any damages, reparation, or monetary loss due to the information contained within this book, either directly or indirectly.

Legal Notice:

This book is copyright protected. It is only for personal use. You cannot amend, distribute, sell, use, quote, or paraphrase any part, or the content within this book, without the consent of the author or publisher.

Disclaimer Notice:

Please note the information contained within this document is for educational and entertainment purposes only. All effort has been executed to present accurate, up-to-date, reliable, and complete information. No warranties of any kind are declared or implied. Readers acknowledge that the author is not engaging in the rendering of legal, financial, medical, or professional advice. The content within this book has been derived from various sources. Please consult a licensed professional before attempting any techniques outlined in this book.

By reading this document, the reader agrees that under no circumstances is the author responsible for any losses, direct or indirect, that are incurred as a result of the use of the information contained within this document, including, but not limited to, errors, omissions, or inaccuracies.

Free Bonus from Silvia Hill available for limited time

Hi Spirituality Lovers!

My name is Silvia Hill, and first off, I want to THANK YOU for reading my book.

Now you have a chance to join my exclusive spirituality email list so you can get the ebooks below for free as well as the potential to get more spirituality ebooks for free! Simply click the link below to join.

P.S. Remember that it's 100% free to join the list.

~~$27~~ FREE BONUSES

- 9 Types of Spirit Guides and How to Connect to Them
- How to Develop Your Intuition: 7 Secrets for Psychic Development and Tarot Reading
- Tarot Reading Secrets for Love, Career, and General Messages

Access your free bonuses here
https://livetolearn.lpages.co/spirit-guides-and-archangels-paperback/

Table of Contents

PART 1: SPIRIT GUIDES 1
    INTRODUCTION 2
    CHAPTER ONE: WHAT IS A SPIRIT GUIDE? 4
    CHAPTER TWO: GETTING IN TOUCH WITH YOUR
    ANCESTORS 15
    CHAPTER THREE: ASCENDED MASTERS AND HISTORICAL
    FIGURES 25
    CHAPTER FOUR: ELEMENTAL BEINGS AND NATURE
    SPIRITS 32
    CHAPTER FIVE: WORKING WITH SPIRIT ANIMALS 40
    CHAPTER SIX: DEITIES AS SPIRIT GUIDES 48
    CHAPTER SEVEN: UNDERSTANDING ANGELS AND
    ARCHANGELS 56
    CHAPTER EIGHT: CONTACT YOUR GUARDIAN ANGEL 63
    CHAPTER NINE: WORKING WITH ARCHANGELS 70
    CHAPTER TEN: OTHER GUIDES AND HOW TO FIND THEM 80
    CONCLUSION 90
PART 2: ARCHANGELS 92
    INTRODUCTION 93
    CHAPTER ONE: ANGELS AND ARCHANGELS 101 95
    CHAPTER TWO: SPIRIT GUIDES BASICS 106
    CHAPTER THREE: ANGELIC SIGNS 117
    CHAPTER FOUR: THE ZODIAC ANGELS 126

CHAPTER FIVE: COMMUNICATING WITH YOUR GUARDIAN ANGEL 134

CHAPTER SIX: CONNECTING WITH ANGELIC BEINGS 144

CHAPTER SEVEN: THE ARCHANGELS OF THE FOUR CORNERS 155

CHAPTER EIGHT: MORE ARCHANGELS AND HOW TO WORK WITH THEM 164

CHAPTER NINE: PRAYERS AND MEDITATION 173

CHAPTER TEN: WORKING WITH SPIRIT GUIDES BEYOND ARCHANGELS 180

CONCLUSION 188

HERE'S ANOTHER BOOK BY SILVIA HILL THAT YOU MIGHT LIKE 190

FREE BONUS FROM SILVIA HILL AVAILABLE FOR LIMITED TIME 191

REFERENCES 192

Part 1: Spirit Guides

The Ultimate Guide to Contacting and Communicating with Your Guardian Angels, Spirit Animals, Archangels, and More

Introduction

Suppose you've ever been interested in the spirit realm. In that case, you may be aware of a theory that claims we all have spirit guides — an embodiment of our higher selves —constantly watching over us. Not only do these guides provide a source of direction and guidance for your life, but they also offer protection from negative entities. For the average person, contact with their spirit guide is fairly sporadic, but there are ways to increase your chances of connecting with them.

There are a couple of advantages to connecting with your spirit guides. As mentioned, there is the practical issue of guidance and protection, but it's also possible that there are healing benefits involved. Another reason this is an endeavor worth looking into is that when you connect with them regularly, you'll receive the simple assurance that they will watch over you. They'll be able to provide you with a higher perspective on life in general.

You'll find that this is a practical guidebook that will take you by the hand and walk you through the process of finding and connecting with your spirit guides. It's a book that is very much needed in today's world, where things are very uncertain, and it's hard to find your way through your life with everything thrown at us by the modern world. You'll learn how to connect with all sorts of spirit helpers, from archangels to spirit animals, guardian angels, and more.

Fortunately, you've chosen just the right book. It's written in clear and simple English, doing away with any terminologies that may make it difficult for those with non-specialized knowledge on spiritual matters to connect with the concepts explained. You'll find that it has enough exercises and practical, hands-on techniques to help you find and connect with your personal guides. Unlike other books out there, this book is particularly concerned with keeping you safe all the way through the process, and not only that, but the things you will learn aren't your regular page-one results on Google. You'll also be pleased to note that the writing is deliberately inclusive, so no matter where you're from or how you identify, you can trust that you will be treated with respect from page one through to the end.

It doesn't matter if you're a complete novice regarding spiritual affairs or if you've been on your spiritual path for many years. In the pages of this book, there is something for one and all, and you're bound to find it a rich addition to your knowledge bank on spiritual matters. Every chapter has some golden nugget of wisdom that could change your life phenomenally if you allow it.

Rather than being a cold, clinical dissection of methods required to make contact with the spirit realm, this book is warm and packed with stories of how ordinary people like you could connect with their guides. People who have had very real experiences with them. Allow their stories to inspire you and give you the faith you need to make it happen for you. If you're ready to make the incredible journey toward connecting with those charged with keeping you safe, loved, protected, and provided for, then let's get started.

Chapter One: What Is a Spirit Guide?

You're never alone. Even when you feel at your loneliest, there's always someone with you, whether you know it or not. There could be one or more beings with you, but there's never a moment when you're left to your own devices. The trouble is that many people don't know how to contact these spiritual friends - deliberately - to ask for their help, and that's what you will learn to do in this book. Who are these friends, ready to assist you in any way they can? They are your spirit guides.

What is a spirit guide? A spirit guide is any being or entity in the spiritual realm who can make their presence known in our world, so they can offer us help, support, insight, guidance, miracles, and protection from harm. These beings will offer their guidance through subtle spiritual means like intuition, dreams, and visions. Sometimes, they can make themselves visible so that you can observe them with your own eyes.

Your spirit guide can take on so many forms, but, in the end, it is helpful to think of them from an energetic standpoint. The form they take on is usually chosen to help you connect with them in the way only you can or to help you glean a specific message that wouldn't strike you deeply any other way. Sometimes they can show up as regular people, with the only telltale signs that they're not regular people being the way they showed up, helped you with something, and promptly faded into the background.

This book seeks to answer the question, how can you connect with your guides deliberately and make communion with them an everyday thing? This question is worth answering because when you choose to become more aware of your guides, you will find that they, in turn, will improve your quality of life.

Spirit Guides in the World's Religions

Most major religions include a belief in spirit guides. Some of them, like angels, are pretty obvious. However, other traditions describe their guides as more subtle and ambiguous entities. In Buddhism, for instance, the concept of spirit guides is known as the "spirit teacher." This source of wisdom can help a person overcome suffering by learning to accept change and relinquish human attachments to material possessions. The "spirit teacher" can guide a person toward enlightenment and help them to develop the correct principles for living a fulfilled life.

In Hinduism, there are numerous spirit guides known as *Acharyas*. These are minor deities that serve to protect people from harm. They also act as divine advisers and teachers for the gods. They're similar to angels in that they do not possess their own form but have unique personalities. Similar concepts are found in Christianity, with the concept of guardian angels and, for the most part, spirit guides that protect people from demonic influence.

In Islam, the angel Jibra'il is considered a spirit guide who helps people develop their spirituality and find inner peace. In Judaism, there are angels known as *malakim*. These spirits also serve to help people to overcome suffering and develop correct principles for living. They can provide a source of guidance and an idea of how they want to be remembered in death.

The possession of a spirit guide is not an uncommon concept in the New Age community. This belief has its roots in 19th-century Spiritualism, which was largely purveyed by people who believed they could communicate with the dead. This remains a popular belief today, particularly among people who practice mediumship or contact spirits to help someone else.

Does the idea of spirit guides sound far-fetched? Well, if you're willing to entertain the notion that humans are capable of communicating with the dead, then how much more logical is it to believe that we can communicate with our own spirits? Although traditional religions may not accept this belief, that doesn't necessarily mean it's wrong. After all, there's no way to prove whether angels and other entities exist in any objective scientific sense. However, when you look at it from the point of view of personal experience and subjective evidence - particularly in the form of meditative or prayer experiences - it is easy to see how this concept can be taken seriously.

Returning to the idea that contact with your spirit guides can protect you from harm, there is some scientific backing for this viewpoint. Scientific studies have found that prayer provides comfort, security, and a greater likelihood of overcoming challenges such as illness or addiction.

The Roles of Spirit Guides

1. **They help you figure out what your purpose in life is.** We all have moments in our lives when we question the purpose of life. We wonder if we're here to do anything specific or if we're only born to distract ourselves until we die. Whenever you're feeling that sense of existential crisis, you can rest assured that having access to your spirit guides will help you understand your purpose in life. They can help you find peace because you're exactly where you need to be. If you want to know what the next step is for you in life, you can trust them to set things up so that you will know just what to do. They help plant you in the right place at the right time to accomplish what you came here for.

2. **They keep you safe and protected.** One of the most common reasons to get in touch with your spirit guides is to ask them for protection. As mentioned earlier, they guard us against negative influences and help us avoid those things that could harm us. From a more practical viewpoint, this means they help keep you out of trouble when you come into contact with people or situations that

could put you in danger. They can also assist you when trying to set up your life for success by helping you steer clear of risk-taking behavior or anything else that might stand in the way.

3. **They provide gifts or inspiration.** It's not a bad idea to ask your spirit guides for gifts or inspiration since this is one of the main functions they're meant to play in our lives. If you're working on a big project or goal, it's usually a good idea to reach out to them and ask them what they think of your chances of success. They can work as advisors in decision-making since they'll have something to say about whether something will work out based on their own experiences. They can also serve as a sounding board for your long-term goals and plans to get a view of your direction instead of just going by your feelings. This can help you stay on course when things turn for the worst and ensure you don't veer off course.

4. **They encourage you to set and achieve goals.** One thing we often forget about is how important it is to have goals in life. Goals keep us motivated since they're meant to be our motivation system. This doesn't mean that, without spirit guides, we'd be left without goals. But it's always helpful to have a little peer pressure and support behind you. Spirit guides tend to be very encouraging by nature. They're great at helping you create big goals and keep you motivated to achieve them.

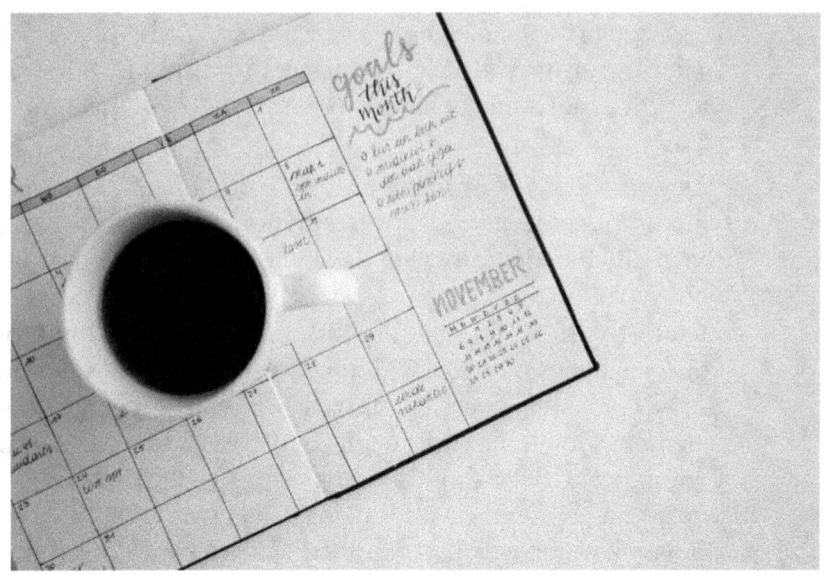

Spirit guides encourage you to set and achieve your goals.
https://unsplash.com/photos/aQfhbxailCs?utm_source=unsplash&utm_medium=referral&utm_content=creditShareLink

5. **They can heal you.** This one is pretty obvious, but it's still important. Spirit guides can assist in healing, both emotionally and physically. This can include relieving stress, reducing anxiety, helping you sleep better, or even curing physical illnesses. This depends on the type of spirit guide you're talking to. For example, suppose you're working with a guide who specializes in healing. In that case, it will be easier for them to help you through your problems than if you were working with laid-back energy who's more focused on socializing. They may also know exactly who you need to see or what information you need to learn to access the healing you seek. This may mean you'll get a message from them to see someone because they think you need treatment for an illness or an injury, even before it happens.

6. **They help you get over obstacles.** Everyone has obstacles in life, and the trick is to find a way to deal with them. If you have a problem at work or a relationship issue, reaching out to your guides can be an effective way to deal with that problem. Guides specializing in heart issues can

provide advice on how to get over your ex, fix issues at work, or help you learn better ways to deal with people in general. This is why ensuring you work with a knowledgeable guide is important.

7. **They can help you to meditate.** It's been said that spirit guides specialize in meditation, and they can be very helpful to those who know how to work with them. Since this skill is one of the most powerful tools available for dealing with any issue, you must prioritize learning how to use mediation to manage your life and heal yourself. Meditation puts you in a state where you're not only able to connect with your guides more efficiently, but you can also accept the spiritual and physical miracles waiting for you to receive them.

Signs Your Spirit Guide Is Around

1. **You feel a constant emotional pull.** You may just be going about your business when you're hit with a very strong emotion that you can't justify. This is one way your spirit guide can reach out to get your attention. The emotion you feel could be so intense that you feel a pain deep in your chest, a wave of giddy excitement, or some strong movement of energy in your solar plexus. You could also suddenly get goosebumps as a result of those strong emotions they create within you. Try to recall whatever you were thinking about, or consider who you were talking to or the situation you're in. They may be trying to tell you something about it. Notice the quality of the emotion as well, and act accordingly. Here's Kate's story: *"I was in the parking lot at the mall about to enter my car when I felt a sudden strong feeling in my chest, almost like pain. I couldn't explain it, but it was followed by a strong urge to go back into a certain store. So, I did just that, and there I found a little girl who had lost her mom and was looking scared. I asked her what her mother was wearing, and she mentioned she'd had a gray shirt with blue jeans. Several people were dressed that way, but I got the same tug in my chest again, followed by an urge to look up. I saw a woman who fit the description, and I just knew it*

was her. The little girl confirmed it, and the woman was happy to be reunited with her kid again."

2. **You see physical signs.** Your guides can also make their presence known through things like signs. This can be anything you could interpret as a sign, like a set of numbers or even words on a piece of paper or billboard. Often, people will dismiss these signs as nothing more than mere coincidence, but that's not the case. This is synchronicity, one of the languages your spirit guides will use to connect with you. They could make you pass by strangers talking about something you were just thinking about, bring your attention to clocks and license plates when they show certain numbers, or wake you up at very specific times during the night. When these things happen, you should know that your guides are near and may have some important information to share with you. You may also notice flashes, shimmering lights, and a presence just outside your line of sight that seems to hover behind you, among other things. Mark says, *"Every time my spirit guides want to get my attention, I tend to see the number 333 or 212. Often, I find that if I pause to recall what I was thinking about when I saw those numbers, the answer to the problem I was dealing with at that moment blossoms in my mind in the form of a picture. I've learned never to take those signs for granted."*

3. **You notice others around you react to your guides.** Someone may ask you if you just felt an odd breeze in a still room or if you heard a sound or something. Normally, you should be able to sense these things on your own, but if you're feeling doubtful about the presence of your guide, they could reach out by making their presence known to other people in the room as well. Gwen says, *"My spirit guides like to have a bit of fun with me and the people around me. Often, I could be talking to a friend, and we'd both get a weird chilly sensation on the napes of our necks. My friends have become sufficiently comfortable to joke about it. When that happens, I often stay still and listen to my inner intuition. There's always a message for my friends and me when my guides show up in that way."*

Your spirit guide is there. You just have to know how to find them. They are always with us and can't be silenced for long periods. If the signs are clear enough, you can feel their presence.

How to Avoid Connecting with the Wrong Spirits

When spirits cross over, they have many reasons for doing so. There are messages they hope to bring up to loved ones or tasks they need to perform. We must treat them with respect and the individual time and attention they require.

However, there are times when a spirit will try to connect with someone who does not want them around for one reason or another. After all, it can be difficult enough for a spirit to find the person they want without being sent on an endless chase due to unwanted connections that the living makes with them, consciously or subconsciously.

Connecting with spirits is not uncommon, but when the wrong kind of spirit comes through, it can be disastrous. You can do the following to avoid connecting with the wrong spirit or to sort things out if you wind up contacting one.

1. **Call a professional exorcist.** If you sense a negative presence, contact a professional who will conduct an exorcism on your person or house. It is important to remove any negative energy present for positive energy to flow freely.
2. **Make sure you have adequate home protection.** Use protective symbols around your house and land if you feel unsafe, and make sure that you do not leave mirrors in front of your bed when you go to sleep so that they don't act as portals for the spirit to invite more spirits to bother you or give you nightmares.
3. **Make personal protection a priority.** Always have a clear mind, stay in a good positive state, and ensure that your spiritual energy is always balanced and in check. Suppose you are feeling unwell or get that feeling that an evil spirit has possessed you. In that case, it is best to immediately

seek help from a powerful spiritual person who is experienced in these matters.

4. **Make sure you get protection from your family and get them to protect themselves.** Family members and relatives may be able to feel the presence of a negative spirit. If this is the case, they may be able to identify it and help you rid yourself of it. They also need to protect themselves by becoming more spiritual and doing things like regular cleansing rituals.

5. **Join a support group.** If you are connected with a wrong spirit and would like to connect with the right one, then join a support group on Facebook or in person, where there is an opportunity for you to share your experiences and stories without fear of judgment. This forum allows you to empathize with people in similar situations and exchange advice to safeguard yourself against negative forces when engaging with them.

6. **Have a trusted person in your life you can talk to about it.** It helps to relieve the burden if you can talk about the problem you're facing with someone who is not only close to you but who will not judge you for trying to walk your spiritual path or making a mistake.

7. **Have a personal relationship with the Divine.** Developing a personal relationship with the Universe or your higher power is another way to avoid connecting with the wrong spirits. The source is light, love, and positive energy; therefore, inviting presence into your life will allow positive energy and good spirits to enter while discouraging negative ones from making their home inside you.

8. **Do some self-examination.** If you are connected with the wrong spirit, then you may want to examine why you contacted it in the first place. Things such as revenge, negative thoughts and feelings, depression, and hurt can lead you toward connecting with a negative spirit. Negative spirits will bring out these traits in people they possess to keep themselves happy. Also, if your connection with a negative spirit is self-inflicted, you could have some issues that need to be resolved on your part. This may include deep-rooted childhood issues or other trauma that has not been dealt

with properly and manifests through unwanted haunting or attacks from a supernatural being.

9. **Don't be alarmed if you do connect with a negative spirit.** Do not be alarmed if you are experiencing anything out of the ordinary and feel everything is fine and nothing is happening. Fearing will feed the negative entity and encourage them to stick around and torment you. When you choose to be blasé about their presence and unbothered, this discourages them from seeking you out to make trouble for you, and they could leave you alone eventually.

10. **Disconnect your energy from the negative spirit.** Visualize a cord connecting you, and then visualize yourself encased in pink light. Let this light cut through the cord that connects you to the spirit. Then, imagine the pink ball of light growing brighter and melting the spirit into nothingness. This exercise should be done from a place of love - not fear - if you want it to be effective.

11. **Ask spirits to leave your property.** If you have unwelcome spirits, it is best not to invite them in. It's not just a case of telling them to leave and expecting it all to be over and done with. You need to ask them to go in a respectful but firm way.

12. **Summon your other spirit guides and ask them to banish this negative spirit from your life.** Simply ask them to take the spirit away, and they will do it, as spirit guides are a source of positive energy, and the negative spirit can't abide by their presence. You can also enlist their help to rid you of the negative entity by asking them to surround you and your property with love and light.

13. **Summon Archangel Michael.** Call upon this Archangel by name and request him to come to remove the negative spirit from your midst. He is an angel who is prompt to answer your calls for help and will not let you down. He will remove the entity with his sword of fire, burning it out of your existence.

14. **Sprinkle salt around your home.** Salt is an energetic purifier. If there's one thing negative entities cannot stand, it is salt.

You can sprinkle it in corners, at your doors and windows, and around your bed. Also, when you take a bath, you should do so with some salt. Envision the salty water enveloping you with a purifying, protective white light that keeps you safe from all harm.

15. **Burn some sage.** Sage has always been used by one and all to eliminate unwelcome presences in a space. Its smoke purifies the energy and makes it incredibly difficult for negative spirits and other beings to stick around. So, consider getting some sage from a new age store and smudge your house, working from room to room. Don't just walk around aimlessly. You have to fix the intention in your mind that you want your home to be free of negativity as you smudge it.

16. **Light a white candle and intend for its energy to cleanse your home.** White is a very significant color. It's a color that attracts positive energy. So, if you get the sense that a spirit you invited isn't who you thought it was, and you want to rid yourself of it, you can light a white candle in each room and let it burn out completely. Set the intention in your mind that the candle's energy will drive away all evil and bring only love and peace into your space. Be aware of safety at all times when working with candles.

Chapter Two: Getting in Touch with Your Ancestors

Ancestors and departed loved ones are some of the easiest spirit guides to get in touch with because you share emotional and blood ties with them. Who are your ancestors? We all have a past. We all come from somewhere, and somewhere on that family tree is a figure or figures near and dear to us. We may not know much about them, but they are there and ready to be contacted through the power of intention.

Your ancestors are spirits. They are entities you may have physically or energetically come from, transcending their physical bodies. Because of this, they are much more powerful than most spirits you will come across. Your ancestors could be the spirits of loved ones, friends, relatives, and others connected to your bloodline or generation before they passed away into the spirit realm where they now reside. They are not only there to offer you guidance and love, but they can be extremely useful when it comes to spell work when trying to influence a situation or the actions of another person or being.

The most important thing to remember when trying to reach your ancestors is that you may not always be able to contact the specific spirit you are looking for. Instead, try reaching out specifically to the spirit of your closest bloodline. You may not be able to connect with a specific loved one, but instead with someone who resembles their personality or looks. Your ancestors know what they are doing, and there is a reason why they have come to you in the form they choose. There may be something you need to learn or a specific message they have for you. If your intentions are in the right place, they will come through. They are here as long as you need them, and nothing could make an ancestor prouder than seeing their family members succeeding in life. You may not always be able to see them, but they're very close to you and can communicate with you differently if you stay open to them.

Apart from their general wisdom and knowledge, there are several reasons why contacting your ancestors can be beneficial to you. They can give you advice on anything troubling you. They have been there and done that. They have seen things we could only dream of and have infinite knowledge about everything in the universe.

What Do Your Ancestors Look Like?

Your ancestors can appear to you in your dreams, dressed just as you'd expect them to have been back in their time. Sometimes they may show up wearing all white or whatever color is most associated with your bloodline on an energetic level. You'll know this color, too, because the odds are while it may not be your favorite color, you may have a strong fascination with it, or people may have strong reactions to you when you put it on.

Your ancestors can also show up as nothing more than energy. However, this doesn't mean you won't be able to deduce it's them. You can tell because they will let you know who they are through intuitive nudges or any other means at their disposal (such as someone randomly talking about ancestry or a book falling and opening to a specific page that talks about ancestors and guides).

Signs Your Ancestors Are Around You

It doesn't mean it's the end of life when we pass away. It's a new beginning, and for ancestors, part of that new beginning will involve their old life somehow. This is why they're invested in seeing how their successors are doing in life, and when they can help, they will. We just need to know how to sense their presence and encourage it. So here are the signs that they're trying to reach out to you.

You dream about them: This is one of the ways you can tell your ancestors want to connect with you. They'll come to you in dreams or as actual nightly visions. Spirits who have passed on favor dreams a lot. The nature of these dreams tends to be hyper-realistic, even more real than waking life. Here's Zoe's story: "My dad passed away not too long ago as a result of the pandemic. He and I had had a rocky relationship as far back as I can remember, but toward the end of his life, he'd tried to reach out to make amends. Sadly, I was a little too proud to let him do that, and I felt too hurt by his past actions to be able to forgive him.

"I remember the last message I sent him was that I'd see him eventually. I had no idea how wrong I would be. When he got sick, I was too far away to do anything, and the lockdowns were in full force. Not a day or night went by after that when I wasn't torn up with guilt. Well, one night, I went to bed and had a dream. I saw him, wearing the whitest outfit I'd ever seen, standing at a peaceful, serene river. He smiled beautifully, looking radiant, and beckoned me to join him. He hugged me, and without words, he let me know it was okay. He held nothing against me, was sorry for how he'd been when he was alive and said he would always watch over me. As I hugged him, tears filled my eyes. When I woke up, my body felt as though I really had just been hugging someone, and I smelled his scent of Old Spice, tobacco, and an odd perfume. Since then, I've been reaching out to him for help and companionship, and he's been very good to me."

You get intuitive nudges to take action right away. This is another common experience that tells you it's your ancestors speaking to you. Say you're wondering how you will get a new car when you can't afford one. Your ancestors could cause you to suddenly desire to go through your spam mail, and you might find a message from an old client who wants you to help them with a project that could incidentally net you just enough money to get the car you'd like. So, it goes without saying how important it is to be in tune with your intuition because ancestral spirits can communicate better with you when you're deliberate about listening. In fact, here's a true story about how Nick could get himself out of a toxic relationship thanks to listening to his ancestors. *"I had hoped for years that things would change, but by the time it became evident to me that my* *partner would always be the same and not make any effort to do better, I was trauma bonded to them. This meant that each time I thought of leaving, I just couldn't bring myself to do that. So, I said a quick, quiet, desperate prayer to my ancestors. It was all of four words: 'Please 'Please set me free.' This led to a series of events where I found out my partner had been unfaithful to me. I wouldn't have found out if I hadn't listened to my ancestors when they told me to call specific people, check specific spots in the house for signs, and so on. I knew what I found wouldn't be enough to convince me to let my partner go, so I said another prayer, 'Please give me the strength to walk away.' Things played out in a matter of days in such a way that whether I wanted to or not, I had to leave. My ancestors led me to a wonderful relationship six months after that. I'm thankful to them."*

Someone says or does something around you that distinctly reminds you of them. Maybe they talk about them, clear their throat just like they used to, or sing a melody that's too obscure for anyone else to know but your ancestor. Here's Shawna's experience of this very phenomenon: "*My mother passed away, and things weren't great where we left them. I had always wondered about what could have been. One day, a friend called me up to tell me about her own mother, who hadn't been good to her either. She told me that her mother had called her out of the blue to say, 'I'm very sorry for never being there for you, but I promise you that from now on, I'm always available to you no matter what.' As she said those words, I felt goosebumps all over me. As if that wasn't enough, the radio I'd had on suddenly went from playing modern music to a song by Tina Turner, which my mother would often sing around the house when we were younger.*" For Shawna, this was clearly no accident at all. She had just received communication from her mother through her friend. That's how the ancestors work sometimes.

They could reach out through animals. If your ancestor had a special animal they loved, don't be surprised if you notice them around you a lot or if they tend to stop and funnily stare at you. You may also suddenly be inclined to have an animal just like theirs or find yourself a sudden parent to one. This could be your ancestors trying to comfort you and show you they still love you and are very present. Sometimes, it may not be actual animals but pictures of them. Many people have stories about how they'd suddenly start seeing cats or owls everywhere they went when they lost a loved one. They talk about seeing them on the television, at the store, or even at work, one of the last places most people expect to run into animals.

Your ancestors can reach out through animals.
https://pixabay.com/images/id-2083492/

Don't assume you never could if you've never had any of these experiences. There are ways to achieve contact with your ancestors, and we'll get to those in a minute, but first, let's talk about how important your family tree is.

Your Ancestral Family Tree

You don't need to know your family tree, as you could simply work with the loved ones you know who have passed on, whether that's a parent, grandparent, aunt, or anyone you had a blood connection with. However, it can be pretty beneficial if you want to work with your ancestors to know your lineage. No mistake about it; figuring out your lineage can be complicated, but it is worth the effort. Fortunately, you can find websites on the Internet that can help you locate your family line and build up your family tree. Knowing your family tree is important because not only can you know the names of the ancestors you want to work with in particular, but also the periods in which they lived and where they originally came from.

The more you know about their place and time, traditions and customs, the easier it'll be for you to connect with them.

Apart from websites like Ancestry.com to help you with your family tree, you can also get your DNA analyzed to learn more about your roots. It may surprise you that you may have much more interesting roots than you once assumed. A quick search on the Internet should show you websites that make it possible for you to get an analysis of your DNA and receive your results. Knowing your roots will help you reconstruct the lives and times of your ancestors so that you can form a stronger bond with them.

Before You Reach Out

Reaching out to your ancestors is an endeavor that should be taken with all necessary precautions. The last thing you want to do is have yourself interacting with the trickster spirit masquerading as one of your own. So, before you begin, we need to cover the necessary things you must do to put yourself in the right frame of mind and spirit to connect with your ancestors.

1. **Have a cleansing bath.** This is no ordinary bath as it is meant to rid you of physical, spiritual, and energetic debris from your body and soul. Working with spiritual matters is like attracts like; therefore, if you carry stuck negative energy, you may be attractive to tricksters and negative entities. For this cleansing bath, simply put some salt into your water and intend that you're cleansed, spiritually and physically. If it helps, you can envision yourself being surrounded by white light as you soak in the tub. If you don't have a tub, simply take a regular bath, and then you can burn some sage to cleanse yourself, or simply sit for five minutes imagining white light burning within and around you, removing all darkness and keeping it at bay.
2. **Create a sacred space for them.** You can do this by cleaning the space you wish to use when contacting them with salt water (to mop the floors and clean any surfaces) or some sage to smudge the area. You can also create an altar by setting up items that you know matter to them on a simple table, before which you'll sit to do your meditation to reach out to your ancestors

3. **Meditate.** Some people like to think of meditation as something it's not. It's simply about maintaining your attention on one thing for an extended time, long enough to allow your conscious mind to relax and access your subconscious and the greater spiritual realm around you. You must find somewhere you won't be bothered for at least ten to fifteen minutes to meditate. Sit or lie down, wearing comfortable clothing, and shut your eyes. Bring your attention to your breath, breathing in through your nose and out through slightly parted lips. After a few breaths, you should start to feel more relaxed in mind and body. Then you can call out to your spirit guides simply by stating you want to be in touch with them or drawing your attention to them in your mind. Meditation should be done daily, not just when you want to reach out to your guides, but as a practice to keep your spiritual senses sharp.

Methods for Getting in Touch with Guides

1. **Make offerings to your ancestors.** When you have set up your altar, you can offer them things you know they'll appreciate. For instance, was there a special kind of clothing they were known to wear? You could put that on the altar. If you know their favorite foods, drinks, and smells, you could also use that. When you've set all the offerings before them, let them know in a short prayer that you're offering these to them to connect with them. Thank them in advance for taking the time and effort to connect with you.
2. **Work with your dreams.** You can connect to your ancestors through your dreams. It's very easy for them to reach out to you through this means. It's not a difficult thing to do. Simply let them know you want to connect with them through your dreams. Set this intention front and center in your mind before you go to bed each night, and they'll eventually show up if they don't during the first night. Also, if you wake up in the middle of the night to pee or something, don't be so quick to open your eyes. Remain in bed and don't move. Relax, and intend to connect with them. You will begin to have visions of them as you lie there

or fall back to sleep and dream of them.
3. **Create an anchor.** This is a gesture you make whenever you want to summon your ancestors, but your situation won't allow you to perform your usual cleansing ritual, creating a sacred space for them and meditation. This anchor is best created when you're in the middle of your meditation or prayers to them. For instance, you could try rubbing your right thumb in a clockwise circle over the side of your forefinger as your personal anchor, or you could pinch your elbow or do whatever you want. When you've got an anchor set up, and you need to reach out to your ancestors or other spirit guides in a pinch, simply doing that makes you more aware of their presence, so you can connect with them better.

Keeping the Connection

So, it's not enough to just connect with your ancestors now and then, and it's best to practice this so that they have more power and presence in your life to do things on your behalf. Here are some ways you can keep that line of communication fresh:

1. **Pick a set time of the day or night that you dedicate to communing with them.** You don't have to always ask for things. You could just say hello now and then.
2. **Do you have things you do every day?** You could pick one of those things and decide you're not going to start it without reaching out to them first. It could be anything from brushing your teeth to sitting down to work at your desk.
3. **Wear something that reminds you of them regularly.** It could be a bracelet, a necklace, or even perfume. Be very intentional about what you choose to remind you of them so that you never forget their significance, and you can keep remembering that you carry them with you wherever you go.
4. **Make a habit of talking to them in your mind.** The more you do this, the more you'll get so comfortable with them that you might even find yourself talking to them aloud. Try not to freak your friends out with this one, so they don't think you're crazy. Conversing with them naturally will make

you feel even more at home, opening you up to their love and blessings. Also, you'll notice that they answer you faster and with clearer messages than ever before.

How to Choose the Best Ancestor Guide to Work With

1. **Pick guides that have gained a lot of wisdom from their experiences in life.** This means it's a smart idea to go with the older ancestors, not those who passed away young. The older they are, the more they've experienced in life, which means they have a much better perspective on your life and can let you know what to do by tapping into their vast knowledge. They've had the time and space to make their own mistakes, so they know better. You can take advantage of that. There's no other pool of knowledge you can tap into that will be like theirs. The fact that they've gone past the physical realm into the spiritual realm also means they can combine the new knowledge of their spirit with the old knowledge from the Earth to give you the very best guidance. They can also comfort you convincingly since the odds are they've lived long enough to experience all the highs and lows of life.

2. **Choose the one who has passed away without giving you grief.** Some ancestors are only there to complain about this life or its people, especially younger generations. These spirits require a lot of energy from living family members and often drain them emotionally. That's not to say that our ancestors are joyless, but rather that they realize that problems, hardships, and heartache are part of life, and they don't linger on this topic once they cross over. They respect all living beings on the planet and just want to help those in need, even if it's only a kind word or a little advice.

3. **Choose one that is empathetic.** Everyone has a favorite relative who is helpful and loving without being overly involved. Even though they claim not to have the energy to help, they come through in big ways or small. Such a spirit is more than willing to share their ideas, counsel, and

understanding with others at any time. Most people who know about these individuals take note of these details and learn from them when in need. Everyone can use a shoulder to cry on, and a guide who is in touch with their emotions and can empathize with you is the best. Don't go for someone who never cared about you when they were alive. If they didn't while they were here, why would they when they're gone?

4. **Choose the ones who have a positive reputation.** If you're still new to this process, you may want to avoid going for people with a checkered past. Maybe they were troublemakers at some point in their life, and their absence from this world meant fewer problems for your family. Don't work with anyone who wasn't known to be good because they may be bad seeds that want to cause more headaches for you and those who are still alive. Besides, these negative spirits are often very demanding and will not let up until you're a mess. These individuals are draining and have an urge to meddle in every aspect of your life, even when it's none of their business.

5. **Choose the ones you have a common connection with.** Everyone has a spirit guide that they're drawn to, but it's important to remember that blood is not truly thicker than water when it comes to this issue of choosing an ancestral guide who is good for you. You may be more comfortable with someone in your family just because they share your last name, but is that enough? If you can't find anyone in your family or lineage worth working with, it's okay to go with a guide who you know would be good to you, even if they're not a blood relative. If you don't have any other connections, you may as well take those who seem happiest to help. They are there for everyone, regardless of age or background. These spirits are always willing to listen and give their insight on whatever topic. As long as they know you're faithful, they will never turn away from your requests for help.

Chapter Three: Ascended Masters and Historical Figures

All about Ascended Masters

Ascended masters are spirit guides who have ascended, meaning they are no longer held back by the karmic cycle of birth, death, and rebirth. They continue their spiritual evolution in the world of spirits, and from this world, they offer their guidance to those of us still on this cycle to help us ascend just as they have. The lessons these masters have for us here on Earth are of a high, strong vibration, and they must also help you ascend on your path.

Once upon a time, having an ascended master for a guide was reserved only for those souls who were well along their karmic journey, but today, with more light and knowledge, it's easy for those who want to connect with them to do just that. Why would you want an ascended master as your spiritual counsel? Because they've been through everything you're going through, and they've learned to overcome it all, which means they can show you how.

When you're ready to wake up from the dream of physical reality, access your Christ consciousness and move on to the next level spiritually, your ascended masters will show up for you. There are many ascended masters available, but remember that not all of them choose to teach. The ones meant to cross paths with you are a perfect fit for your unique life and experiences, which is why working with them is the best thing you can do for yourself.

Stories about Meeting Ascended Masters

This is Layla's story: *"Here's what happened when I met my ascended master, who told me I could call him Mariel. My ascended master came to me in a dream, during a time when I had decided that I would be more dedicated to my spiritual walk. I never dreamed of having one, so I was very surprised to find that I did. He explained that he had been assigned as my guide for my whole life and would continue to be with me on my spiritual path until the end. He told me that he'd come at this time to help guide me on my journey out of my body and into the light. He described his role as being to help me overcome any barriers I may have had that prevented me from taking the next step toward enlightenment."*

Here's an account by Starr about how she got experienced her meeting with her ascended master when she was just a young girl: *"When I was a young girl, I had a very stern, gentle teacher. He taught me how to breathe and hold my body in a way that strengthened me and prepared me for life. He appeared to me many times, usually in the company of my mother or grandmother, who were both deceased. He would appear when I was alone and wanted to know something he happened to want to teach me. I would always sit in a chair, and he would appear before me. He was a tall, thin man with long black hair, piercing blue eyes, and surrounded by a white halo that surrounded him like misty clouds. With time, he would appear to be alone, as I no longer needed my grandma or mom to assure me that my experiences were real and safe."*

How to Connect to Your Ascended Master Guide

One thing you must remember about ascended masters is that they're non-conditional. In other words, they won't place any requirements on you when working with you. They understand the importance of free will and will honor yours. In other words, you will not get any intervention unless and until you ask them for help. Before attempting to connect with them, please make sure you use the preparation methods from the previous chapter to be ready and safe. Now, let's talk about how you can reach out to them.

Say a simple prayer. Your prayers don't have to be complicated. You can just say "thank you" to them, whether for something good you've experienced or something you'd like them to do on your behalf. A prayer of thanks is more than enough to connect with them, as thankfulness is a state of being that is pretty high in vibration. Make sure you feel the appreciation coming from within you as you thank them for their love, guidance, support, protection, provision, and all else you want to express.

Meditate on their picture. If you know your ascended master, you can meditate on an image of them if you've got one. This is actually the best way to do it if you're a beginner because you're already connected to these people through emotions. You will feel more sensation when doing this – which is a good thing. As a bonus, if you happen to be working with a group of ascended masters, looking at their pictures during meditation will help you distinguish their individual energies one from one another. You can ask for the different masters' help in specific situations or their guidance about life. Don't know what they look like? Check out the next suggestion.

Meditating on your ascended master guide's image can help you connect with them.
https://unsplash.com/photos/HS5CLnQbCOc?utm_source=unsplash&utm_medium=referral&utm_content=creditShareLink

Connect with them in your dreams. Before you go to bed, intend to meet them in your dreams. They will show up as long as you continue to make that intention clear, and you keep an open mind to them. It's helpful to thank them as if they've already made themselves known to you in your dreams because that will make them show up faster.

Notice the signs you get in your physical reality. To help you understand just what this means, here's an experience that Jesse had: *"Just as I was sitting here in my chair, writing this, I noticed a door in my house open and shut all by itself. This isn't the first time it's occurred, and it's not like it's a faulty door or anything of the sort. So, what's going on? I know my ascended master is here with me, and looking at the time, I can tell that it's exactly one minute until to when I should be meditating. This tends to happen simultaneously, like clockwork, and I know it's no coincidence because I had a dream where I saw my ascended master open and shut a door and then tell me to note the time. Since that dream, they've always used that medium to remind me when it's time to do some spiritual work."* What strange things are happening around you? Start paying close attention.

Channel the masters through writing. This is another way to connect with them, and it can be done in an internal dialogue or journal. When you're in a quiet place, ask them for help. Then write down what they say to you as soon as possible after you get the information you seek. In other words, don't worry about how silly it may sound out loud – just do it. Flow with it. Trust is essential if you're going to get anything that's worth something from them. If nothing shows up immediately, just know it will after some time. If you can no longer hear anything in your mind, or the thought impressions they send you stop coming through, read out loud what you've written so far, and add more things to it on your own about what you've learned from what they shared.

Connect with the masters through painting. This is another type of art-based channeling where you release your creative spirit in the process. Pick up a paintbrush and draw whatever you feel guided to draw by the ascended masters. You will immediately feel their presence and be able to communicate with them. If you can't figure out what to draw, close your eyes and ask the ascended master for help again. As with any other type of channeling, you can also release what you've drawn into the universe so that it may be used in a way that's good for everyone or to manifest a specific intent you may have.

Keeping the Connection to Your Ascended Master Guide

1. **Learn how to lucid dream.** Connecting with these guides is easier when you have better control of your dreams.
2. **Learn how to astral project.** Astral projection will help when they need to show you things on the other side of the planet or a different universe entirely, rather than working with you through your subjective dreams.
3. **Meditate often.** When you meditate, you will inevitably become more sensitive to their energies, making them reach out to you with any information they feel you need to know, which will benefit your life tremendously.

Historical Figure Guides

Historical spirit guides are exactly what they sound like. These are historical figures who once lived on Earth and are no more. You can work with them as guides too if you want to. Suppose you notice that you're particularly drawn to a certain historical figure. In that case, the odds are that you will find it easy to connect with them if you want to.

Before you connect with a historical figure, you need to do your homework to know all there is to know about them. You should look into where they were born and raised, what they were known for, what it was like living with them, what they liked and disliked, and anything else you can learn about them. Looking for the perfect historical figure guide for you is to consider where you're at in life right now and then think about the sort of energy that could help you along your journey as you research different figures. You'll have no trouble knowing when you've spotted the right guide for you as you do this.

Here's how Dmitri connected with Mozart as a spirit guide. *"I was desperately seeking motivation, and for a long time, making music no longer gave me the same joy it used to. When I learned I could work with great musicians who had passed on as guides, I was beyond ecstatic. I chose to work with Mozart as I'd always loved his sound and originality. Since then, I've had no regrets. He's helped me find my spark again, and now my music has added dimensions and quality to it that I never in my wildest dreams thought I could achieve."*

How to Connect with Your Historical Figure Guide

As always, please remember to practice safety first. Prepare your body, mind, and space for connecting with these guides before you get into it.

Figure out who you want to work with. As you learn about great people who did amazing things in different aspects of life, think about how your life could parallel theirs and check in with your heart to see who calls out to you. You'll know who it is because their name will either jump out at you, you may dream about them, or you'll stumble across information that confirms they're the ones you should be working with through synchronistic events like seeing an article on them, or hearing about them.

Use items they would always carry as totems to draw their energy. For instance, if a figure you've chosen always had a pipe with them, you could buy one and keep it in their honor or place it on your altar when you want to connect with them.

Meditate on their essence. Simply relax during your meditation, and then bring their names to your mind. You can also conjure up a picture of them in your mind and then sense their energy enveloping you fully as you meditate on them.

Work with them in dreams. The beautiful thing about dreams is that they make it easy for you to connect with those who have passed on, no matter how long ago they died. So set an intention before you go to sleep that you'd like to connect with them. If you have a question for them, fix that question in your mind, and quietly affirm your thankfulness to them in advance for showing up and giving you the answer you seek.

Visit historical sites connected to them. When you go to these sites, you should get a sense of their energy and be able to connect to them deliberately. You'll find it's smart to look into the historical figures in your own hometown, as it means you'll have easy access to their old homes or favorite locations that they were known to visit often. You're likely to leave an energetic imprint when you often go or live somewhere. So, going to these places will make it easy for you to connect with your guides. With time, you may not need to make these visits as they become more familiar to you, which means you can work with them whenever and wherever you want.

Chapter Four: Elemental Beings and Nature Spirits

Elementals and nature beings aren't human in any way, though they can actually take on the form of humans if they want to. They are the spiritual essence of the natural elements and the rest of nature. Let's begin by discussing elementals.

Elemental Beings

There are four types of this kind of being, and each is connected to one of the four classical elements; Earth, fire, air, and water. Gnomes are considered earth elementals. Salamanders and sylphs are fire and air elementals, respectively. Mermaids are water elementals. It's important to note that there's a fifth element known as ether, akasha, or spirit, which we as humans possess. You should know how elements affect us if you work with elemental beings as guides.

When you're working with water, you'll be much better at feeling your emotions, expressing them, and being a loving person. When you're working with air, you're more in touch with your creative side, able to create wonderful art and find the beauty in all things. When you work with the earth, you want to deal with grounded matters and create a world where things last and have value. When you work with fire, it's all about power and will. It's a very expansive element, and its sheer intensity makes it possible for you to deal with anything that keeps you from being your authentic self to the fullest.

The following is Venus's account of how she connected with an elemental being names Gaia: "After learning about her, meditating on her energy signature, and then going to sleep with her on my mind, I dreamed of a tall woman who was like a nature goddess and who looked like she was very wise. She said to me, '*You're doing just fine on your journey.*' She gave me the information that I needed. She then said that I should align myself with the four elements to find balance and harmony in life. She also permitted me to ask her in the future if I need help with any of my other elemental guides."

Signs an Elemental Is Calling to You

1. **You keep having dreams about their element.** If you're always dreaming of water, fire, earth, or air, there's a chance that's because you have a special connection to the spirits of these elements. They could inspire you to take concrete action toward reaching out and developing a mutually beneficial relationship with them.

2. **You feel like you're undergoing an awakening.** There's a reason why many people experience physical symptoms when their elemental being is calling out to them. While it's not guaranteed every time, it's worth paying attention to your body and feeling what is happening to it as you become more aware of your internal energy in relation to the surrounding elements.

3. **You start to become obsessed with the element.** If you are outside; it's a stormy day. The lightning is making your hair stand on end, or you're in the shower thinking about water as hard as you can. Strange things start happening around you; this is a sign your elemental guide is trying to communicate with you. You may also experience intense physiological phenomena, such as an increased heart rate or vision alteration.

4. **Strange visions are assailing you.** In dreams, people's elemental guides can be as varied as those they guide. Some dreams they show me are more animalistic and feral, while

others are more ethereal and spiritual. Just remember that it is your elemental spirit guides you are seeing, not something else in the dream world. If you feel someone is trying to penetrate your subconscious mind or consciousness deeply through dreams and visions, this is a sign that the spirit wants to speak with you somehow.

5. **You feel energy signatures or bursts of overwhelming sensations.** Some people experience a rush of energy near certain geographic locations that resonate with different elements. For example, if you're walking along the beach in Santa Monica, and it's a beautiful sunny day, you might feel like your heart is being pulled toward the ocean. If this always happens, this may be a sign from your spirit that the element of water is calling to you.

How to Connect with Your Elemental Spirit Guide

1. **Ask your elemental guide to contact you.** You can ask your elemental guide to contact you in any way. You can call out to the elements, for example, through prayer or writing a letter summoning them to you.
2. **Trust that they will come.** Your spirit guides won't show up until they know they're trusted and will be welcomed by you. They may offer you a message when you're ready for them to. These messages can profoundly affect your life and the world around you.
3. **Examine your dreams.** If you have dreams about spirits or entities, pay attention to the element being called to you. You may dream of the nature of these spirits, where they call from, their appearance and traits and qualities, and even their purpose for contacting you.
4. **Listen to your body.** Just as the Earth speaks to you, your body will often speak to you in energy sensations. Listen to what it has to say.
5. **Get out in nature.** Being away from the city and going into nature can be a great way to connect with your spiritual side. And, when you do get outside, seek out the element calling

you the loudest.

Being around nature is one of the ways to connect with your spiritual side.
https://unsplash.com/photos/ndN00KmbJ1c?utm_source=unsplash&utm_medium=referral&utm_content=creditShareLink

6. **Meditate in nature.** I truly believe there's no better place on Earth than the vast landscapes of planet Earth, especially when they're wild and untamed. One of my favorite things is meditating in the mountains after a long day of hiking or camping. By reaching out with your energy to the elements and the Earth, you open up the energy coursing through our planet.

7. **Say prayers to the elementals.** You can always pray if you aren't comfortable meditating or writing to your elemental spirit guides. Praying is a way to express your desire to communicate with them. Your prayer doesn't have to be fancy or formal. It's literally just a conversation with the elementals, telling them what you want to and listening out for them to see if you get any answers on the inside or in your physical world through synchronicity and signs.

Honoring Your Elemental Beings

1. **Leave them gifts in nature.** Just as you leave gifts on the altar for your gods, you can offer things to your elemental guides as a sign of gratitude. These may be special items such as traditional foods that are special to the element they are associated with, or natural and handmade items made by local artists and craftspeople.
2. **Observe nature.** Being in nature can offer many opportunities to connect with the elements, from being out in the woods, trekking through a mountain, or being at a beach.
3. **Perform ceremonies.** There are many ways to honor the elements, from small handmade offerings to rituals in nature and celebrations of traditions such as Celtic fire rites.
4. **Greet your spirit guides.** Do this with respect and love. Remember that you're talking to your fellow travelers on this journey through life, and make an effort to be friendly and knowledgeable about who these elements are.

What Are Nature Spirits?

Nature spirits are non-physical entities that live in and around nature. They exist in their own realm and have the trust of the elements. Many people confuse nature spirits with elementals, but there are differences. Elementals are spirits that come from the elements. Nature spirits are part of the elementals, either as helpers or a conglomeration of other elements, depending on their role in spirit work and helping humans. They are made of etheric matter, and they help to sculpt reality.

Here's how Darren connected with a nature spirit in a tree in his backyard: "*I had been working on connecting with spirits in my life. I kept getting this strange feeling each time I saw the image of the apple tree from my backyard in my mind repeatedly. So, one day I decided to go into my backyard and greet it, and that's when it happened. I felt this strange energy come over me. It was as if I was talking to an old friend I hadn't seen for a long time. The energy was very welcoming. Whatever it was, it asked me if I wanted to* work with it, and I accepted. Ever since then, I've been doing that tree's will and working with nature spirits in general."

Riley found a deep connection with the spirit of their local pond. Here's their story: "*I first felt drawn to the pond over a year ago and have come back several times since then, always trying to get a better feel for the spirits in this place. I've meditated a few times here and found that their energy is strong. The last time I was here, I brought some of my friends, and we all felt the presence of something spiritual. But, with so many people, it was hard to know what was what. Nature spirits are not used to large crowds and may have sensed us as more of a threat than anything else.*

"*I'd been thinking about this pond for a few days when I finally decided to come here again by myself and with my journal in my hand. I felt a strong urge to sit down on the bank of the pond and write and meditate. My eyes scanned the surface, and I saw something in the distance. The closer I looked, the clearer it became that it was a swan, and it didn't appear to be swimming at all. It was moving flawlessly through the water with its head held high toward the bank where I was sitting.*

"*Then, I saw something else. The swan had another being with it, and this other being was coming up near the surface of the water toward me. This creature's head was also held high, and it seemed to be looking at me. I wanted to see its face, but as it came closer, there was some kind of mist that blocked my view. I got a message, like a block of thought in my head, about how it was a nature spirit. I right away got into my meditation and connected with it. The lessons I learned from it changed my life forever.*"

Signs a Nature Spirit Is Calling to You

1. **You get a feeling of warmth around you when you're outside in nature.** In addition to warmth, some people feel a sense of fellowship and acceptance from nature spirits. Others feel as though they are literally surrounded by the element they want to meet.
2. **You will see signs in nature.** The natural world is the unique way that nature spirits communicate with humans. They may appear as a rainbow, their symbol, or as a beautiful animal or plant.

3. **You feel a sense of peace, love, and harmony.** Nature spirits are very interested in helping humanity, especially the planet Earth, which is all about growth and evolution.
4. **You have visions or nightmares about nature.** Some people say that nature spirits influence their dreams. Some people even claim to have had experiences where they saw the actual beings of nature around them as if they were real. Others speak of a spirit guide who comes to them in their dreams and gives them directions via the dream world.
5. **You smell a plant or flower that isn't around you.** Some people report being able to smell nature even when they're not out in it. Some smell plants, while others report smelling animals like squirrels or birds.

How to Connect with Your Nature Spirit Guide

After preparing your mind, space, and body to connect with these guides, you can proceed with getting in touch with them.

1. **Pray to your spirit guide.** You can ask the spirits anything you want to. In the woods, you can lie down in a place of worship and say prayers to them. Again, praying is simply telling them anything you want to. You can ask for the spirit of a tree or any other nature to lend you a hand in your life. It can be an amazing experience, especially if you already have a relationship with that nature spirit.
2. **Ask them specific questions.** Some people believe that nature spirits are good listeners and will answer their questions. Other people say that not all nature spirits know everything. Either way, it's a good idea to be prepared with a few questions with answers that have always eluded you because these beings are wise and willing to help you all the time.
3. **Get out in the woods or other natural environments.** If you want to connect with your local nature spirits, this is the best thing you can do. Getting out in wooded areas, areas with water and sand, or where you can build a fire, and studying nature, will bring you closer together with these spirits.

4. **Have a feast in their honor:** Some people believe feasts to nature spirits are a great way to bring you closer to them. They may ask for a small offering or simply want you to enjoy the food and drink in honor of them.
5. **Meditate.** This is another method of connecting with nature spirits of the woods and other areas for those who can't get out into the natural world because life gets in the way sometimes.

Honoring Your Nature Spirit Guides

1. **Become a vegetarian.** Many nature spirits are vegetables or animals, so becoming a vegetarian is a powerful way to honor them.
2. **Drink tea.** Some people believe that by drinking natural, herbal teas, you can gain the powers of the nature spirits of those plants.
3. **Wear crystals.** Going out into the wilderness, it's a great idea to wear crystals on your body to attract nature spirits and create harmony with them for any other purpose you might have in mind.

Chapter Five: Working with Spirit Animals

Spirit animals are perhaps the most well-known type of spirit guides. But what is a spirit animal? According to Native American legend, a spirit animal guides its human counterpart as they navigate through life by showing them their strengths and weaknesses. Certain animals are known to have this effect on some people more than others. For example, some people may associate with a wolf, while others may see a bat as a sign of protection.

The idea of spirit animals is not new and has been around for centuries — but the list of spirit animals is constantly changing along with modern culture and beliefs. When looking for the answer to the question of whether your spirit animal is real, you must understand that we are all blessed with a spirit animal. The signs they give us allow us to learn when to expect changes in our lives and give us a key to understanding certain situations surrounding us. Without proper guidance from your spirit animal, you may be in some type of misfortune or even make mistakes. Your spirit animal is always there for you and will never leave you.

Whether you realize it or not, your spirit animal may affect several aspects of your life. It is important to know that your guides are always there for you, and it is up to you to acknowledge their presence in your life. Your spirit animal can be an excellent source of strength, happiness, and insight whenever you need them the most.

The great thing about spirit animals is that they are supposed to help you, not hinder you. They are always with you and will guide you along your path. However, to keep them happy, you must be respectful to them and learn how to listen to their advice. They will often be happy and helpful and guide you along the right path if you show respect. Obey their advice, and your life will be filled with both happiness and insight.

Let Oliver share how he learned about his spirit animal and reached out to it: "I was looking for an animal spirit to work with, but I didn't have anyone in mind. So, I asked my spirit guides for help. They told me about the animal best suited for me, and it was a bear. I believe this animal spirit chose me as his guide and has been with me every step of the way. I started out by making my ancestor's totem pictures and placing them in my home." Oliver already had some experience working with his guides, so it was easy for him to ask them for help, and they came through. You can do the same thing, too.

Karen has a story about how she found her own spirit animal. Here it is: "*Here's how I connected with my spirit animal. I was in a car with my family driving home when I decided to take a moment to reflect on my life. I was riding in the backseat, staring out the window, and feeling self-conscious about how depressing it had all become with how each day could easily be described as an exhausting battle of constant struggles. It seemed like all it would take for me to reach hopelessness was one more thing going wrong. So, I asked the universe, "Is there anything you can do to make my life better?" I then got a very unexpected answer in my heart; "Connect with your spirit animal." I wanted to know what it was, and right then, I saw a big billboard with a swan on it. I just knew right then and there. My spirit animal was a swan. Ever since I began working with the swan, so many miraculous, marvelous things have happened in my life.*"

Naomi discovered her spirit animal was a lion. Here's how: "*Here's how I discovered the lion is my spirit animal. I always thought I was a cat person, but one day as I was daydreaming in class, on the brink of sleep, I realized I would rather be a lion.*

I always wanted to be in the limelight, doing something great and special. But the dreaded voice in my head kept telling me that I would fail, that I wasn't good enough to do these things. Then I fell asleep briefly, and there was a vivid flash of a beautiful lion standing before me gracefully and powerfully. It said to me, "I'm with you. You will find success in all you do if you work with me now and always." I wasn't a spiritual person before, but after that day, I chose to look into spirit animals and began working with my lion's energy. I have had no regrets since then."

Spirit Animals, Totem Animals, and Power Animals

Where your spirit animal is a guide, your totem animal is your essence. It's your energy or who you really are. Your power animal is the energy you draw upon from the spirit realm when you need strength or help with something in your life. You can ask this power to remain active all through your life or only to be activated when you're in trouble or need to help someone else.

Signs Your Spirit Animal Is Calling to You

1. **You have dreams where you see them all the time.** Dreams can be very useful to help you learn about your spirit animal. For instance, if you have loads of dreams where an animal is chasing you, it may not necessarily be a nightmare. It could signify that your spirit animal wants to get your attention.

2. **You see them in your everyday life.** If you see your spirit animal during your day-to-day activities, it's a sign that they're around and watching over you. If you see an animal out of the corner of your eye, and it disappears, this could also mean that your spirit animal is trying to get you to notice them.

3. **You hear them even when they're not around.** People have reported hearing their spirit animal's sounds without any animals being around or right in their ears just before going to bed or waking up. You may experience this yourself when you start connecting with them actively.

4. **You feel them.** Suppose you feel as though something with primal, animalistic energy is watching over you. In that case, it might be a signal from your spirit animal. It might be difficult to recognize at first if they're nearby, but once you do, listen carefully because they'll start talking to you differently.
5. **You sense a shift in your life.** Have you felt an overwhelming urge to take action in some area of your life, powered by primal instincts? It could signify that your spirit animal shows you the best path to take.

Can You Have More Than One Spirit Animal?

Even though it seems like it would be difficult to have more than one spirit animal, the answer is yes. Although this may seem strange, people have been known to have several spirit animals in their lives. It can help you know that you have more than one support system in life, and you don't have to be alone.

Some people may have one as a "primary" spirit animal and others as the secondary one. This can depend on various factors, such as your needs at the time. For instance, if you are having trouble with someone in your life, you may be guided by a spirit animal specializing in protection and defense. This is just one example, but you could find that a variety of spirit animals guide you during your lifetime in different situations. It's all about finding the one that best suits you at the time and in whatever situation you happen to be in.

It's also important to be aware that having multiple spirit animals doesn't mean that they are supposed to make their presence known equally. Some may show up more than others because this is required at a certain time in your life. So, not every spirit animal you have needs to show up often. Some people's lives may be easier than others, which may mean that the nature of your spirit animals will vary.

A spirit animal is a spiritual guide you come into contact with and then bond with them, or you can be born with them. They are like guardian angels who have watched over us since we were kids.

They can be described as a higher intelligence within us, and they can help us in case we need some guidance.

How to Find Your Spirit Animal

1. **Use your intuition.** The best way to determine your spirit animal is to use your intuition. You can feel them when they are around, and you will know the exact moment they are there, which can be really helpful. If you feel that a particular animal is the one you need to be with, it can be very helpful to speak to them. I suggest you try and get in touch with them if you are having any major problems in your life, so they can help guide you.

2. **Try meditation.** Another way to figure out your spirit animal is by going on a meditation retreat. Wherever you are, your spirit animal will make itself known to you. You mustn't overexert yourself when meditating because this can cause the spirit animal to leave once again or not even show up. When meditating, it's good to breathe in the scent of any nearby animals and then picture them in your mind. This opens up the communication process that helps meet your spiritual companion.

3. **Take a walk in nature.** Going for a walk in the wild can be incredibly helpful if you are feeling lost and confused about what to do. Getting out of the city and into nature can help you feel more at peace with yourself, and this can make your spirit animal physically or spiritually come forward to help you. You may find they will speak out loud when they are around, or they may just give you a sign that lets you know they are there.

4. **Do a reading.** You can also do readings to figure out your spirit animal. There are variations of doing a reading that can help you determine what your spirit animal is. A lot of native cultures will use methods like this. Some psychics will just know what your spirit animals are without even having to do any sort of ritual.

5. **Connect with your elders.** Another way you can learn about your spirit animal is by talking to the elders in your family or community. They may be able to hint at what it is, or they

may even tell you that they know exactly what it is. If they don't, I suggest trying the other techniques before speaking with them again.

How to Connect to Your Spirit Animal

1. **Visualize them.** A good way to connect with your spirit animal is by visualizing them. This can be done through meditation or just thinking about them from time to time. If you want to know yourself better, then I suggest you try this technique, as it helps open up communication with the spiritual side of yourself.
2. **Ask for signs.** When you feel your spirit animal is close by, do what you can to find out their name and what they represent. This can be done in two ways: thinking about them and asking for a name to pop into your head or asking them to appear in front of you somehow and ask for their name.
3. **Learn about their characteristics.** What do spirit animals represent? Each animal has their own unique characteristics. Learning what they represent can help you connect to them more easily.
4. **Talk to your spirit animal.** Sometimes, our spirit animals can help us out in times of need, and they are capable of offering advice as well. This can be done through meditation or thinking about them when you need help.
5. **Ask them for help.** If you are ever in need of guidance, then I suggest you call out to your spirit animal. They can help you when you are in a jam, but they will only come if they think it is necessary. You should also write down what you need help with and then burn that piece of paper. This can help clear the path to communication between the two of you, and it will make it easier for your spirit animal to talk back to you.
6. **Don't force the connection.** Quite often, people will try to forcefully connect to their spirit animal to get proof that they exist. This is not the best way to go about it, as it can make your spirit animal leave you, or it can make them become

more hidden from you.
7. **Have faith.** That is important if you have faith in your spiritual companion and know they are there. They will eventually make themselves known to you, and if they are not in your life yet, then don't worry. They will show up when the time is right.
8. **Ask your spirit guides to show you your spirit animal.** Your spirit guides will know which animals you're supposed to connect and work with.

How to Honor Your Spirit Animal

You must show some respect and honor your spirit animal in much the same way you care about the well-being of physical animals on earth. These spirit animals have been assigned to take care of you and deserve to be shown some appreciation. It only makes sense to honor them and treat them as more than just helpers and messengers. Doing this will create a powerful bond between you, and they will be able to serve you better in turn because of your devotion to them.

Many people choose to name their spirit animals and tattoo them on their person. This practice comes from Native American cultures and has been adopted by many groups, including African American heritage and spiritual practitioners like Celts, Druids, Ancient Egyptians, etc. Here are other ways you can honor your spirit animal.
1. **Make offerings to your spirit animal.** You can honor your spirit animal by offering them and putting them in a place where you will see them. Offerings can be anything from food to clothing and more.
2. **Connect with them just to say hello.** I would suggest using meditation or just thinking about your spirit animal occasionally. Your spirit animal is there for a reason, so honoring them is necessary if you want them to stick around. You shouldn't wait until you need help to reach out
3. **Consult your elders.** Your elders may have some information on how to go about honoring your spirit animal better. Talk to them and see what they have to say. They are

often very knowledgeable about finding our animal guides and other spiritual beings.
4. **Wear jewelry that reminds you of their presence.** Make it something unique that reminds you of the animal alone.

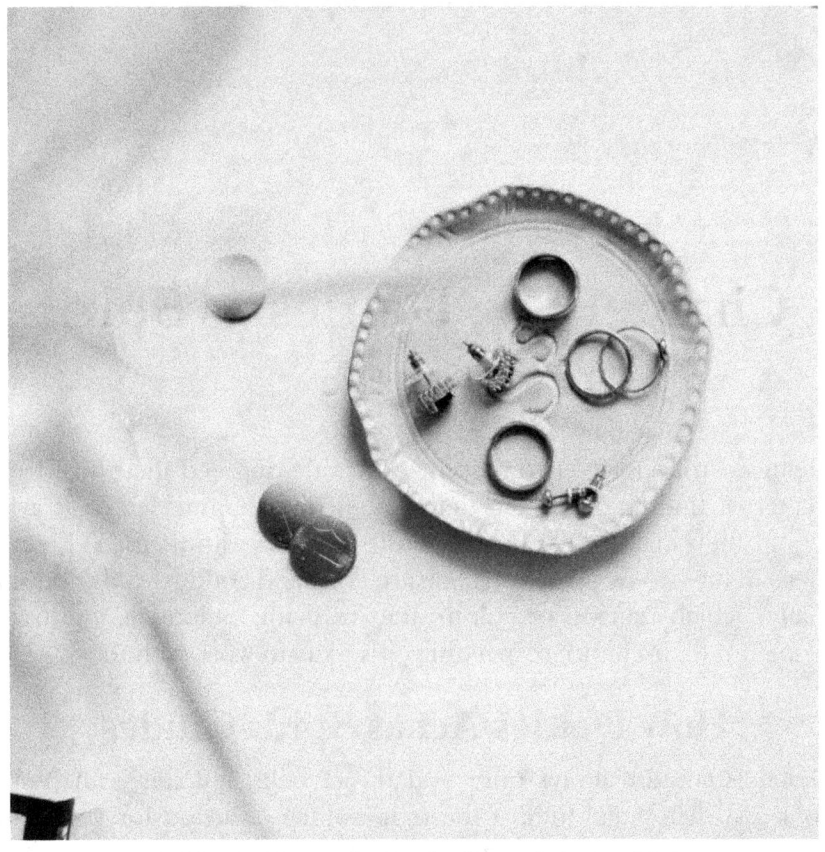

Honor your spirit animal by wearing jewelry that reminds you of their presence.
https://unsplash.com/photos/ECr_8nuXpBA?utm_source=unsplash&utm_medium=referral&utm_content=creditShareLink

Chapter Six: Deities as Spirit Guides

Deities can also act as your spirit guides if you need them to. It's a matter of finding out which deity you're most connected or drawn to and then making it your mission to connect with them. Who are these deities, to begin with? They are gods and goddesses. It doesn't matter which religion or culture they're from; as long as you treat them and their culture respectfully, it's okay to work with them.

How Deities Act as Spirit Guides

Deities may not always offer you direct help, but they can point your guardian angel toward the right course of action for you, and your guardian angel can, in turn, communicate that to you. It's important to note that deities aren't a permanent part of your spiritual army of guides. They'll show up and help but then be on their way. More often than not, when you call on them, they will send you a message or the answer you seek through some other spirit guide.

The thing to note about gods and goddesses as guides is that they can help you whenever you want, but often, *it's just easier to work with your other spirit guides.* This isn't because the deities can't or won't help you, but because they're more inclined to intervene personally when you're in particularly dire straits. You can turn to many deities, like Amadioha, Horus, Kali, Selene, the Buddha, and more. You just need to do your homework to figure out which of them you resonate with the most.

Nikita shared her story about connecting with the goddess Luna as a spirit guide: *"I've always been a huge fan of the moon, and when I realized how connected it is to everyone, I decided to focus on her and see what would happen next. It started with just me noticing a lot of synchronicities surrounding the moon. Then, I began seeing the goddess's face framed by the moon in my dreams, but I wasn't sure if that was just a coincidence or not. Then, one day when I was meditating, I noticed that she was speaking to me. She was saying, 'You are always connected to the moon. It is part of who you are.' I don't see her often and only choose to work with her when I have a very troublesome situation. She's lovely to work with and has unmistakable power."*

Signs a Deity Is Around You

1. **You notice a lot more synchronicity in your life.** You realize that the universe has been conspiring to work with you and not against you, and this causes a sense of empowerment in you. You notice way more happy little "coincidences" that are a little too perfect for you to think of as just random events in your life.

2. **You feel more positive and uplifted.** You realize that you're surrounded by love, and it feels good. Your moods are more positive, you smile more, and the world just feels like a better place to be because of all the love you feel. You know that higher powers are here to support you, making you want to be a kinder, more compassionate person.

3. **You hear unusual noises or voices that others can't understand.** The voices are usually soothing and gentle, but they don't always make sense to you at first. This is because they sometimes come to you in other forms - like sounds or images - instead of words. Usually, you'll experience these phenomena in deep meditation or when you're on the cusp of sleep and being awake.

4. **The spirit world becomes more accessible to you.** Deities can help you get in touch with your guardian angels if you're curious about what they have to say, and it's easier for your

other guides and angels to help you in general. They can make you more aware of the world beyond the veil.
5. **You start to experience spiritual gifts.** You may suddenly find that the things you say tend to come to pass or that you have visions or flashes of the future. You could develop Clairaudience, Claircognizance, Clairsentience, Clairvoyance, or Clairgustance. You may notice you can pick on what people are feeling and thinking more or that your desires are starting to manifest at what feels like warp speed. All of these result from the intense energies of the deities around you, who naturally lend their power to yours to make you a little more than human.

Which Deity Should You Choose?

To figure this out, you must expose yourself to as many deities as possible while checking in with your gut to see which one pulls at you. Some people just know right off the bat; for others, it will take more time and research. Either way works.

Another way you can discover which deity you should be working with is to look at your ancestry, trace as far back as you can, and see who exactly your ancestors used to worship when they were still alive. You could then make that god or goddess your go-to spirit guide for when you need that extra spiritual muscle to back you up.

If you can't trace your lineage for some reason, it's not a bad idea to check in with a professional, genuine psychic. The psychic will be able to read your energy, note any other god-like energies that are attached to you or that you resonate with, and give you an answer about who you should work with. Don't be shocked if they can't figure it out on the first visit, though. It may take some time.

You could also use a pendulum to help you discover which deity to work with. Get a pendulum from any new age store or an online store. Next, write out the names of every deity of interest to you. Figure out which way your pendulum swings for yes and no by asking yourself questions to which you already know the answers and noting how the pendulum swings in response. When you know which swing is yes and which is no, allow the pendulum to swing over each name on your list, and then note the response you get. Trust that that's the deity you should work with as a guide.

Another thing about deities is that each has specific symbols and correspondences. For instance, if you're drawn to Hecate, you should know that her symbols include crossroads, keys, torches, dogs, and the triple moon. So, if you've seen these symbols around you, the odds are that's the goddess to work with. The same applies to all other deities. Also, consider that if the god or goddess in question is calling you to work with you or responding to your request to work with them, you might notice their symbols tend to show up more often than usual in your life. This is a sign that you're good with them, and they are with you.

Remember that it's a good idea to make offerings to your deity. Some deity guides will require more rituals and offerings than others to provide you with whatever you seek, so when you're doing your homework on deities, you should also keep this in mind so that it's easy to appease them.

How to Connect with Your Deity Spirit Guide

Remember what you need to do before you attempt to connect with your deity. You should cleanse your body with salt water and/or sage, cleanse your space, and clear your mind with meditation before you begin to reach out to them. All this will keep you safe and help foster a deeper connection between you and your chosen deity.

1. **Meditate on them.** Once you've decided which deity you want to work on connecting with, meditate. Once you're deep in meditation, you'll feel a shift happening inside of you. Don't be surprised if your deity begins to address you directly through blocks of thought. They may also present an image to you or create a distinct sound that you perceive within you, which has a very observable effect on your body and mind.

2. **Visualize yourself sitting with your deity and having a conversation.** Imagine they're right there with you, and let them know what it is you'd like them to help you with, trusting that they will deliver the answers you seek. This works especially well when you're trying to get guidance on

something that's troubling you.

3. **Put something sacred belonging to your deity in a place of honor.** If you can, get something that belongs to your deities, like a statue or a painting. Place it somewhere in the room where you spend most of your time so that the visual reminder helps you regularly connect with your spirit guide. The object could also be an heirloom that you inherit from your family. There are plenty of things to choose from because deities are connected to virtually every culture on this planet.

4. **Pray.** Prayer is a powerful way to connect with your deity when you don't know what else to do. Praying will help you feel better and happier, which is the entire point of connecting more with the spiritual realm.

5. **Work with them in your dreams.** If you use either lucid dreaming or astral travel, try focusing on your deity while you're dreaming. This creates a very powerful connection to them on a spiritual level.

6. **Use charms, talismans, and other objects with meaning to you.** If there's something that's particularly meaningful to you connected to your deities, like a pendant or even just a little rock with a nice shape or aesthetic quality to it, see if it helps you connect with your spirit guide.

7. **Make offerings and perform rituals.** This is especially powerful if you have a deity you've been worshiping for a long time and feel indebted to them. A ritual offering can be as simple as lighting a candle in their name or as complex as an entire ceremony. The offering is what binds the connection between the two of you, so don't let it go to waste. This offering is payment for all the good that they do for you in your life.

Performing rituals can help you connect with your deity.
https://unsplash.com/photos/x5hyhMBjR3M?utm_source=unsplash&utm_medium=referral&utm_content=creditShareLink

Ritual to Reach Out to Any Deity You Desire

1. Sit in the center of the room you usually spend time in.
2. Light a candle, preferably one used for a ritual for the deity you're trying to connect with. You can also use incense if you have it or just play some music.
3. Perform your first intention. As you begin, glance up at the image of your deity and ask them to help you with whatever it is you want to know from them.
4. Perform your second intention. Then, after you've finished meditating, take the time to thank them for being there with you, and ask them to help you in any way they can.
5. Take the time to truly enjoy the feeling of your deity being present within you. It may be a subtle feeling, but they are always there if you just begin listening for them.
6. Make an offering to them in exchange for their service. For example, you could offer her dirt from a crossroads or a key in Hecate's case.

When it comes to the intention you set for your rituals, you must ensure you're certain about what you want. Words are very powerful, and the deities will hear anything you wish them to, so if you wish for something that's not pure of heart, they may take that as a command and act on it unexpectedly.

Honoring Your Deity Spirit Guide to Maintain the Connection

1. **Always remember them.** This is the most important part. Don't let your connection with them fade because you don't see a direct benefit to it in your life. They're there with you in spirit and want to work with you as much as you want to work with them.

2. **Use the gifts they give you.** When they give you something like a dream or a message, take advantage of that gift by learning from it and applying it to your life in any way that feels right for you. If you gave a friend gifts and they never opened or used them, odds are you'd be upset and quit giving them anything. It's the same principle here. Make a point of using the gifts you're given.

3. **Write them a thank-you note.** Regularly writing down the things that you're grateful for and thanking your deity works wonders for this connection because, even though it's not a direct connection, it creates the mindset that you'd like to maintain a good relationship with them and not take them for granted.

4. **Worship them in your mind.** We all know that the mind is an important part of the spiritual experience. Take the time to imagine what it would be like to have a relationship with your deity and form a gist of their personality and preferences. This will help you see where you could work on improving your connection with them.

5. **Keep photos of them where you can see them and be reminded of them.** Sure, this might be considered a little more "new age" and not everyone's cup of tea, but if you have a picture of your deity or some sort of physical representation of them in your home, this is a great way to

keep them in your life even if they're not physically around you.

6. **Make offerings and sacrifices.** Sacrifice is an important part of any relationship with a deity - unless you're the type who doesn't like to be indebted to anyone else. Suppose you've done something that displeases your deity. In that case, you can make an offering to them in your mind, or even if you have done something that they are proud of, you can make an offering to them so they know how happy they made you.

7. **Dedicate a space in your home for them.** This is the most important thing you can do to connect strongly with your deity. Take the time to set up a spot in your house or apartment where you can do this. It doesn't have to be anything special, but it should be somewhere they can watch over you as you go about your day and involve something that feels familiar to them - maybe a small statue or something along those lines.

Be patient and persistent. The path of spiritual learning is a long and winding one. Just because you can't regularly connect right now doesn't mean it will not happen. Keep at it, and don't give up. You'll eventually find your groove.

Chapter Seven: Understanding Angels and Archangels

Angels and archangels can be very helpful spiritual allies, and you're about to find out just how you can work with them in this chapter. Certain spiritual beings have very high vibrations, working only with the energies of truth, love, and appreciation. They're not held back by anything that keeps us restricted in the physical world, and they have various assignments and purposes in our lives. Whenever you get mired in low-vibration emotions like hate, fear, anger, and so on, you can turn to these guides to help you feel more like your authentic self once more. You have to give them permission to do what they must to steer you where you need to go.

What Are Angels?

Angels are the highest divine energy beings on Earth. They're so much more than just spirit guides. They're light beings that work within the very core of our souls, guiding and assisting those experiencing spiritual growth. Their purpose is to serve the highest good and justice of all living things, and they do this by teaching people all that they need to know about love and consciousness. They're much more powerful and important than our materialist concept of an angel suggests.

You see, these spiritual allies are guardians we need in our lives to keep us on the right path by standing up for those who can't do it themselves. They're the ones who actually help you make the transition to your next life, so it's in your best interest to work with them regularly. Angels are all thought to be good, loving beings that work for the greater good of the whole human race. There's an endless list of angels out there that is impossible to mention here in one chapter, but the important thing is to do some research and see which one resonates with you the most, checking in with your intuition.

Where Do Angels Come From?

Everyone who knows anything about angels and archangels will tell you they come from the highest point of pure Divine Love. They're the ones closest to the Source Energy of the Universe because they work with this energy daily. When we allow angels to work with us, we become more focused on love and light and start letting go of our fears and troubles because we know it doesn't matter in the grand scheme of things. Our angels always guide us, ensuring we're doing what needs to be done. Because they're so advanced compared to us, they know what's best for us, even if we aren't aware of it.

Do Angels Have a Gender?

When you take a look at the many religious texts that talk about angels, you'll notice that, for the most part, they are described as men. However, this isn't always the case as some of them are women, too. Those of us who have encountered angels in our daily lives know that they come in both genders and in whatever form you find easiest to relate to them in. For instance, Gabriel is a special kind of angel known as an archangel, and he can appear to us as a man or a woman, depending on the situation. The thing about angels, though, is that there are times when they'll show up in a way that makes it difficult and even unnecessary to figure out their gender.

The thing to realize about gender is that it is mostly an earthly concept. In other words, angels do not operate based on the earthly rules and customs we have in place for ourselves, which means they can show up however they want to when they decide to make an appearance on our plane. One might then want to ask, do the angels pick specific genders based on the goals they want to accomplish here? Or is the perception of their gender down to the beliefs and convictions of the people they appear to?

When you check out the Quran, Bible, and Torah, you'll notice that these beings are mostly referred to as predominantly male. However, an interesting bit of scripture in both the Bible and the Torah indicates these religions recognize female angels. Check out the book of Zechariah, chapter five, verses nine to eleven, and you'll note that these scriptures talk about a couple of female angels who raised a basket and a male angel from whom Zechariah received an answer to his question in that passage.

You should also note that angels have energy specific to each gender for specific functions on Earth. Doreen Virtue wrote the Angel Therapy Handbook, and she talks about the fact that while they don't have set genders as their spiritual beings, they do have certain traits and strengths that give them energies you can deduce as very masculine or feminine. For instance, Michael is an archangel known for offering protection, a role primarily thought of as masculine. Then you have Jophiel, who is about beauty, a concept traditionally considered feminine. Despite this, it is important to note that gender-wise, the spirit realm has far more variety than we've already discovered here on Earth.

How Many Angels Are There?

There are as many angels as humans, if not more. It's pretty hard to tell how many exist, and considering that more and more humans are being born every second, it's a fool's errand to figure out how many angels are assigned to each one of us. It's even more pointless when you consider that we could have multiple angels performing different functions on our behalf.

Angelic Hierarchy

There are nine known classes of angels in existence. Note that when it comes to spiritual entities, they go through various cycles of existence, advancing from one level to another, which is why there's a hierarchy to begin with. The higher the rank, the older and wiser the angels, and the closer they are to the energy that creates and sustains worlds. Let's take a look at the rankings.

The seraphim are the highest-ranking angels, and they're known as spirits of love. Everything they do is rooted in the will of the Divine and nothing else. They are also known as the burning ones.

The cherubim are next in line. They're in charge of ensuring a sense of balance and harmony regarding all spiritual consciousness. This is why they're called spirits of harmony. These beings have learned what it means to have Divinely inspired wisdom and knowledge and to recognize the will of Source Energy in one and all.

The thrones are angels who are very aware of Divine Will, in all people and situations, even in what seems less than ideal. They understand that all boundaries and responsibilities have been set in place by the wisdom of the Divine and should not be questioned. They show the Source's brilliance by upholding its will.

The kyriotetes are known as spirits of wisdom. They are all about the expression of Divine Grace and will inspire you to be aware of the infinite possibility that's around you. They're also known as "dominions," in charge of the lower-ranking angels. It's rare to find them mingling with humans. Instead, they'll do their work for you by using a lower-ranked angel as a proxy.

The dynamis are called spirits of motion, and they're well aware of that which needs action that creates change and sustains life. They're all about miracles, and they're known as "Virtues" since they know the connection between having the will to act and the courage to follow through on what needs to be done.

The Elohim are known as spirits of form because they are in charge of all matters involving the incarnation of life on this planet. They have access to the grand blueprint of the Master Architects for every soul, and they're well aware of the precise points in time and space for you to achieve certain milestones meant for the evolution of your soul.

The archaea are spirits of time, and they are the ones who handle the seasons and cycles of the universe and each being. Sometimes you might hear them as "Principalities" or spirits of personality. It is their task to make sure humanity evolves spiritually on schedule.

The archangels, who we shall soon discuss in detail, are known as spirits of fire. They're in charge of whole nations or collectives of human souls, and they're to space what the archaea is to time. They work as go-betweens for the people and Consciousness or the Divine.

The angels are the final ranking here, and they're the ones we're closest to as humans. Their job is to help us become more aware of our lives and to figure out what it is we came here for, what we must fix by way of karma, and how to attain knowledge of the true nature of reality through dharma. We can work directly with them; we all have at least one angel looking out for our well-being, helping us figure out our consciousness and find the divinity within.

More on Archangels

What is the difference between Angels and Archangels? People tend to use the terms angel and archangel interchangeably, but there's one important difference you should know about. Archangels are much more powerful than the average angel because they're in command of the angels surrounding you daily. For example, Archangel Michael is an archangel who serves as a guardian for the whole human race. He works with his army of angels to deter all evil from entering our world, and he's one of the top angels that people have been able to connect with.

In the Judeo-Christian angelic framework, you have the following archangels as the most important ones:

- Archangel Michael, the warrior
- Archangel Raphael, the healer
- Archangel Gabriel, the messenger
- Archangel Jophiel, in charge of beauty
- Archangel Ariel is in charge of animals and nature
- Archangel Azrael, overseer of death
- Archangel Chamuel is in charge of peace in relationships

In Islam, you have the following major archangels:

- Mikal, the provider
- Jibril, the revealer

- Izra'il, in charge of death.
- Israfil, in charge of the final judgment of man

In Occultism, you can call on any of the traditional Judeo-Christian archangels. The idea is that archangels don't have free will, so you can invoke them simply by calling their name and asking them to do whatever you need to be done.

How Angels and Archangels Act as Your Spirit Guides

1. **They keep us safe and protected.** We only have to go back to the Bible in the story of Jacob to know that angels are there for protection and guidance. The most notable instance of angelic protection is when God sent his angel Raphael, a healer, to save a young Tobias and his father from death.

2. **They guide us.** Another important thing we should know is that angels are there with us at all times. They're the ones who give us love and inspiration, and they guide us through the dark days of our lives. They'll always let you know when you need to know if someone is a good person.

3. **They inspire us.** Another thing that angels do is inspire us. When we're down in our emotions or in a bad mood, we can turn to our angels for assistance to get out of that mood. They're the ones who can help us turn things around because they know everything that's happening in our lives. They're the ones who tell us to move forward no matter what. They can also provide insight and advice, so you know that everything you do is the right decision.

4. **They provide spiritual support.** Another thing that angels can do is get spiritual support for you, keep you on track in your life and encourage you when needed. They're the ones who tell you to do everything in your power to make an impact on this world.

How to Connect with Angels and Archangels

1. **Work with your spirit guides daily.** Even if it's only for a few minutes, you can. Your angels and archangels are there to help guide you in the right direction. They can show you what to do and where to go at certain points in your life. They're ripe with wisdom and knowledge, but you must be open enough to hear their guidance. Many people get frustrated when they don't get the desired results, but they need to learn how to be more patient. Our angels are great teachers, so we shouldn't give up on them so easily when they teach us difficult lessons.

2. **Let your angels guide you.** It may be hard at first, but you must learn to trust your guides. They're there for a reason. Follow their lead, even when it doesn't appear to make sense to you. They will take you to a place that could be even better than wherever you wanted to go originally.

3. **Say prayers to them about whatever you need.** Don't just have these beings come into your life and expect them to fix everything on their own. You still have to work with them every day, so you can learn how to get the guidance you need from them. They're always looking out for you, but you have to give yourself to them for them to show you the way, and the best way to achieve this is through conscious prayer to them.

4. **Feel gratitude for your angels.** One of the most important things is to feel a deep sense of appreciation for your guides. When you do this, you're sending out a clear message to the Universe that you want more of the same. The better way to do this is through prayer, just like when you pray to God.

5. **Get rid of all your limits.** Many things will hold you back from connecting with your angels and archangels, but the best way to do this is by having an open mind and being receptive to their guidance.

Chapter Eight: Contact Your Guardian Angel

It is said that everyone has a guardian angel assigned to them at birth. Whether it be a specific person or a more abstract entity, this being will serve as the individual's greatest ally. Angels are said to be able to appear in many forms and to have different duties depending on the person that they are assigned.

But what exactly does an angel represent? The word "angel" means messenger. This may seem like a simple definition, but there is much more here than meets the eye. When Westerners think of angels, they often imagine a being with wings and halos. But this does not accurately reflect the range of beliefs about angels in other cultures.

In Eastern thought, for example, an angel is usually considered to be body-less or even to have several bodies at once. Rather than wings, angels may have long hair or many hands. They also vary in terms of their assigned duties. Some may be messengers while others are warriors, and yet others are servants.

Westerners may also avoid having angels assigned to them before birth and simply believe that angels exist independently, perhaps on some higher plane. But most cultures do not separate their guardian spirits from the world in this way. Unlike Westerners, many Eastern thinkers believe that angels have always been a part of the human world, present on Earth from the beginning of time.

What Is a Guardian Angel?

Angels are considered powerful beings that often inhabit a higher realm and can affect the world below. The ancients believed that they brought them gifts after death. They also sometimes protected humans from dangers, including illnesses and natural disasters. In this sense, they were considered somewhat like guardians or protectors.

They are thought to be able to affect the world in general. Most cultures believe that angels can relax their presence if they like or take on human forms if they want to. But in some cases, they also act as soldiers and messengers. Their duties and purpose vary from culture to culture. But whatever they do and however they appear, they are almost always depicted as benevolent beings who protect the deserving. Even in the case of cultures that don't believe in guardian angels, angels are still assigned to people in the afterlife. These are known as guardian angels.

This is because all humans have souls. A soul is an invisible entity that is unique to each person and carries with it all the individual's knowledge and identity. Souls are also thought to be powerful spirits that can move freely through time and space when released from the physical bondage of the flesh. It used to be thought that the soul was formed at conception. Then, in the 12th century, a monk named Thomas Aquinas argued that it was created at birth. In the 19th and 20th centuries, doctors discovered that around the time of conception comes a special moment when the sperm and egg are most closely joined and can start to carry out their mission. For this reason, some people believe that angels do indeed intervene directly with their help at this stage in their lives.

The medieval theologian, St. Thomas Aquinas, argued that each of us has a guardian angel to watch over us from birth. Some people believe that this angelic being stays with us throughout our whole lives, protecting and guiding us from afar, while others believe that we are assigned new angels at various points in life.

Angels can appear in many forms to help protect the vulnerable and set them onto a path toward the good. They may appear to us as angels, but they may also appear in any number of different forms. For example, many believe that guardian angels can appear as animals. In some cases, these animals are those that are most sacred to the guardian angel's target. So, a cat may be the form chosen by an angel whose charge is a person who loves cats. At other times, the animal form selected by the angel may have no special significance to its charge at all.

Teaching about guardian angels seems superfluous to some people since so much of this information is readily available on the web, in books, or through other media sources. But the tradition of teaching children about their guardian angels dates back to the end of the 19th century. A cardinal in Turin, Italy, is said to have assigned children a specific angel to whom they could write letters with their questions and fears.

Though stories of guardian angels are more widely known today in connection with Christianity, this tradition has its roots in Judaism, which was known as Mal'akh Degadol or "The Great Angel." In fact, most ancient religions believed wholeheartedly in the existence of guardian angels. For example, Arabs believed that an angel named Azrael watched over newborns from birth until death or entrance into heaven. Zoroastrians believed that a spirit known as a Fravashi was assigned to each individual at birth and stayed with them, watching for their well-being as they grew up and helping guide them to heaven. Muslims also believe that everyone has an angel assigned to them at birth. No matter what your religious disposition, the fact is that angels represent a connection to the divine.

Assigning people guardian angels continues to be common among more modern religions, including Islam, Judaism, and Catholicism. However, this practice is not exclusive to any one religion. A guardian angel may be assigned to an individual at almost any stage in their life, even as they grow up and go through different development stages.

Can You Have More Than One Guardian Angel?

There's no denying that many people believe they can connect with their guardian angels and have done so throughout history. In fact, ancient texts contain numerous references to people who claimed they encountered supernatural beings and were guided by them through difficult times in their lives. But the question is, how many of these angels can one have?

There seems to be no limit to the number of guardian angels we can have. Some people say they've had several guardians at once. One person claimed that her guardian angels simultaneously appeared as three real-life beings. Some people have said that every aspect of their lives, from the time of their birth to the things they do in life, is monitored by several guardian angels.

There's no limit to how many guardian angels you may have. Some believe that you can have multiple guardian angels and that each one has an assigned task to protect you in a specific area of your life. Others say several entities work as one, looking after your daily needs and then switching off on different days. You might also have several guardian angels, but they all work with the same purpose to look out for you fairly throughout your life.

Stories about Guardian Angels

Ali's story: "*Here's how my guardian angel helped me to pay my rent. I had been working a stressful job, and on top of that, my landlord decided to increase the rent after I had been there for over a year. I did not have enough money to pay the increase, so I risked losing my apartment. The only way for me to avoid this was for me to find another job. So, as I meditated for two nights about when I would be evicted, I asked my guardian angel for help with the rent. What happened next was astonishing. I started to have feelings that I was going to get a job, a better-paying one. My phone rang, and my friend mentioned that a place was looking for someone with my particular set of skills and that it was urgent. They were going to hire me because my friend had shown them some of my work, and they were impressed. I got a nudge to ask for advance pay, and they were* more than happy to give it, which meant I got to keep my apartment."

Tomiwa's story: "I had been terribly heartbroken from my last relationship, and for about a year or so, I just stayed away from love. Eventually, though, I began to feel a yearning within me to connect with someone romantically, but I didn't want to repeat the same cycle as I did in previous relationships. I sat in meditation night after night for a week, making my intentions to find true love very clear to my guardian angel. One day, a friend invited me out to a party, and I turned them down. However, my guardian angel appeared to me in my dream and said, 'Go to the party and party hard.' I took that as a sign to say yes and have fun. Turns out, I met the love of my life at that party, and we've been together five years. Still going strong. It would never have happened if my guardian angel hadn't been on hand to help me, and I hadn't reached out to them either."

Liza's story: Here's how my guardian angel saved me from being mugged on the street. Last night I was walking on the street, and a man appeared in front of me. He raised his hand as if he was going to hit me, but before he could make contact with my head, a bright white light emerged from behind him.

He was shocked by it, and his hand went down immediately to his side. The light then moved toward me and encircled my body. I could feel something warm moving around my body and then down into the earth below me. I felt myself being lifted off the ground and carried upwards to who knows where.

The whole time, I could hear the man who had tried to accost me calling out to anyone who could hear him, asking what that light was doing there and where it had come from. I stood rooted to the spot, confused and a bit shaken but otherwise unharmed. I heard a soft voice say to me, "You're safe now." If you'd asked me where the owner of that voice was, I really wouldn't have been able to tell you because it was only the man and me on that silent, lonely, poorly lit street. That's when I looked down at my feet and saw the man who had tried to mug me lying unconscious where I had once been standing. I knew then and there that I'd been kept safe by my guardian angel. To this day, I do not take the connection I have with my angel for granted. They've done so many awesome things for me that it's truly hard to keep track of it all."

Signs Your Guardian Angel Is Near

1. **You hear your name being whispered in your ear in the middle of the night or early in the morning.** If you've ever experienced this before, and it left you frightened, don't be. This is likely your guardian angel trying to let you know that they know who you are. They know your struggles and needs and are more than happy to assist you. They call your name to help you realize the truth that you're never alone, even at your worst.

2. **You see a bright light in your room.** Many people believe that when you see this, it's your guardian angel calling for your attention. They want you to know that they're always watching over you and can be seen by you if you wish.

3. **You hear someone call out to you during the day while doing your thing.** In the past, people have reported hearing angelic choirs singing and whispering in other languages. These signs are indications that your guardian angels are near, trying to get your attention and let you know they're present.

4. **You feel angels around.** Do you ever feel like someone's standing right behind or above your shoulder? This is a common sign of them trying to get your attention.

5. **You have dreams of talking with your guardian angels.** Some people regularly dream of their guardians, insisting they're real. This is a sign that you've successfully connected with your guardian angel, and they're trying to communicate with you on the other side. They may want to tell you something important or warn you of something coming around the corner.

6. **You start to notice more synchronicity in your life.** It's said that when you're connected with your guardian angel, there are more synchronicities than ever before in your life. These experiences can include conversations, seeing signs and messages, hearing voices, or seeing images. Sometimes they can be coincidences that aren't really significant on their own. Other experiences are very real and significant

Ways to Contact Your Guardian Angel

Today, there are many practices that people go through to establish contact with their guardian angels. Let's look at some of these methods.

Meditation. Meditating on your guardian angel's energy or connecting with them is more than enough to help you establish contact and begin working with them. You could fix an image of them in your mind as you breathe with your eyes shut in meditation. Alternatively, you could chant their name in your head or out loud or keep your eyes open while focusing on a picture of them if you can draw or paint them. To use meditation to contact guardian angels, first, you will need to decide on your work's specific intention and outcome. You may want to ask the angels for protection from harm, healing from a disease or condition, guidance, and direction in life, help with a career choice, etc. You will then want to connect with your own emotions and commit to yourself that you will do what it takes to achieve your chosen outcome. After this, you can then sit in meditation, breathe, and try to open up your heart and mind to feel your angels' presence.

Channeling or mediumship. One of the most popular methods for contacting guardian angels is said to be mediumship or channeling, a practice in which people believe that they can use their mind or body as a channel for communicating directly with spirits from another realm. The medium channeling process usually involves an individual sitting in a darkened room and channeling thoughts and images projected through their spirit guide's hands. These messages may be delivered through movement, sounds, speech, colorful lights, or even bodily tics.

Prayer. Another popular technique for communicating with guardian angels is through prayer, a common practice for many cultures throughout history. The practice of prayer is generally understood as a spiritual concept, as it involves putting one's thoughts into words and physically speaking to the spirits of the heavenly realm. This is done by speaking to the angels in their minds or out loud, reading prayers out loud, or praying silently. Sometimes, people request permission from their guardian angels to pray aloud on behalf of others.

Chapter Nine: Working with Archangels

It is known that archangels have a lot more power and dominion than angels, and they all have their assigned purpose given to them by the Divine. For instance, Michael is charged with protecting one and all, Raphael is the one who heals, and Gabriel is very helpful when dealing with communication matters, passing along clear messages, and so on. So, in this chapter, we'll take a look at the roles played by each archangel and explain how they can help you in your personal life. *Note: Remember that some are gendered as female and some as male, but it's notable that different belief systems use different genders for some angels. We've used the most common gender for each archangel listed below.*

Archangel Michael

This is the one archangel who is recognized in the sacred texts of Christianity, Judaism, and Islam. This angel is a protector and will always go to war against all that is evil. Archangel Michael is a very powerful being. As long as you have a pure heart and good intentions, he will definitely fight for you when you need him to. He is all about preserving truth – and cannot stand it when people get away with wickedness and injustice to the undeserving. When you get in touch with Michael, you will find his energy is bold and unmistakable. When he communicates with you, he does so with clarity, so you can't miss his message.

Signs Archangel Michael Is Present

You get help when you're in trouble. The divine dispatches this archangel to help you whenever you're in a tight or desperate situation that feels like a real crisis. Many people know you can call on this archangel whenever you're in trouble, and you'll get help immediately. It doesn't matter what you need protection from. He never shies away from lovingly coming to your aid.

He also has an energy that seeps into you, infusing your body, mind, and soul with a sense of calm even in the face of danger. He'll fuel you with the strength to handle whatever comes your way and the courage you need to handle things. Some can actually perceive his aura when he comes around. It's a lovely shade of royal purple, reminiscent of cobalt blue. Others report hearing his voice with their actual ears rather than on the inside.

Regardless of how this archangel shows up, it's often unmistakable when he's in the building. You will see actual evidence, as he's big on making it clear that he's around. You'll also find that there are times he will choose to communicate through your intuition.

You feel a sense of reassurance. If you're in a pickle and need to feel encouraged, Michael will turn up if you call on him. You may notice you're getting an image of him in your head or that you feel a warm, comforting sensation when he shows up. All of these serve to reassure you that you're not alone. He also shows up to comfort those who are about to pass on to the afterlife.

You're driven to accomplish your life purpose. You'll find this archangel is invested in helping you organize your life and boost your productivity levels. You'll know he's with you when you notice that you're leveling up your skills, which helps get you where you need to be. He will help you be more consistent in your efforts.

He will guide you in your dreams. He will sometimes appear in your dreams to give you the guidance that you seek on any matter. Often, you'll know he's there by the appearance of flashes of light.

Archangel Raphael

He is one of the most popular and well-known archangels among Jewish people. He hasn't just been mentioned in the Hebrew Bible but also in later writings as well. His role is to heal and protect people, animals, and even plants. When seeking healing, you can call Archangel Raphael for assistance. This archangel will heal you from both physical and emotional pain. He'll even help you get rid of your fear.

Signs Archangel Raphael Is Present

You feel lighter, happier, and calmer. When you're feeling really stressed out, depressed, or afraid to get up in the morning, this archangel will show up to give you the energy boost that you need. He'll clear and energize your body and mind, making you feel brand-new. His light will fill you with positive energy and the hope that things will be okay.

The presence of the Archangel Raphael will allow you to feel happier and calmer. . https://pixabay.com/images/id-591576/

You notice that something in your life is changing for the better. If it's been a while since something good has happened to you in your personal life, this archangel will make sure he's there to help guide you through this period. He wants to help you reach your full potential, live your best life, and work out any problems you may face. He will come up with a solution that works perfectly for you at the moment that you need it most.

He guides you in your dreams. When he's around, this archangel will appear to you in your dreams to guide you on matters of the heart. He'll tell you how to get back into a better love relationship or patch things up with someone important to you. He knows the right words to say so that everyone can have a perfect outcome.

Archangel Gabriel

This archangel has been mentioned in many popular movies and books. He is represented as being both powerful and beautiful. He is a messenger from God and a healer who will help you recover from hard times.

Signs Archangel Gabriel Is Present

You are inspired to put things into motion. This archangel will help you get started with the action you want to take in your life - whether that means starting a business or making the changes that will turn your dreams into reality. If you're having trouble making decisions, this angel will make sure that you take the first step toward what you've chosen. She knows you can take control of your life and make it amazing, and he wants to coach you in your pursuits.

You get a sense of hope. You feel inspired by this archangel's presence. He loves helping those who are down and out or feel at a dead end in their lives. He knows exactly how you feel when things aren't going your way, so you can tune into his energy and feel good about yourself.

He guides you in your dreams. This angel will guide you in your dreams to help you make the right personal and professional decisions. He'll also tell you how to overcome your fears and get over your obstacles.

Archangel Jophiel

This archangel is in charge of beauty in all its forms, positivity, and creativity. He teaches us how to use our hearts and minds to see the good in others and in ourselves.

Signs Archangel Jophiel Is Present

You feel inspired to follow your passion. You have a burning desire to make your abilities known, whether that means starting a new business, performing on stage, or writing a book. This archangel will show you how you can accomplish all of those things with your natural talents, which are meant for more than just general creativity.

You feel happy. You find yourself doing things that make you smile - even if they're small things, like buying flowers or baking a cake. This angel helps people recognize their worth by helping them find joy in their everyday lives.

You enjoy making others feel good. This archangel will show you how to help others feel better about themselves. He loves taking the time to teach people how to enjoy the simple pleasures of life.

Archangel Ariel

This archangel is in charge of nature and animals. She inspires you to be closer to nature and help animals and the environment. She is there to help you connect with all living things.

Signs Archangel Ariel Is Present

You feel a strong connection to nature. This angel will help you do things that will make you feel closer to the natural world. You may spend more time outside or encourage your family and friends to connect more with the Earth. You don't have to be a vegan or an extreme eco-warrior to tap into her energy; this angel simply wants you to appreciate nature.

You want to be kinder to animals. Whether it's adopting a new pet or working on behalf of animal rights, this archangel will show you how you can make the world a better place for animals. She's there to help you decide to do the right thing for these creatures who don't have a voice of their own.

You want to live more healthily. If you're having trouble sticking with a health plan or eating healthy meals, this angel will inspire you to make it happen through your own willpower. She knows that it takes hard work, determination, and perseverance to be successful in anything you do, but she'll help you through the tough times by reminding you why it's so important for your life.

Archangel Azrael

This angel is in charge of death. He guides people to the afterlife, making sure those who die are ready for their transition.

Signs Archangel Azrael Is Present

You feel at peace with the future. This angel encourages you to rest in your final days and be at peace with what life has had to offer you. You may find yourself reminiscing on your life, which allows you to appreciate the good times and leave them all behind, making your transition easier. You may also cling to the past and have a hard time leaving it behind, but this angel will guide you into thinking about where life might go and help you stay on track.

You are dealing with a death or loss. This angel will give you a sense of peace and closure so that you can move past your grief. He knows it's not easy to deal with loss, but he'll give you the courage and compassion you need to heal.

You feel like life is worth living. This archangel will help you keep pushing forward when life seems hopeless. He knows how hard it can be to keep going when things continue to seem like a struggle, but he'll help guide you toward your goals without giving up hope for better days.

Archangel Chamuel

This archangel is in charge of peaceful relationships between one and all. He brings harmony to people who are struggling with discord.

Signs Archangel Chamuel Is Present

You feel more connected to others. This angel will help you feel less alone and more like you belong in the world. He will help you connect with others and show you that everyone is on your side, even if it doesn't seem that way.

You forgive others. Anyone who someone has ever wronged can tap into this archangel's energy. He encourages us to let go of our anger and resentment to find peace with the ones we love or even forgive those who have hurt us in the past.

You have a new outlook on life. It can be hard to see the good in others when you've been angry or hurt for so long. When this angel is around, you'll feel motivated to start fresh and see the beauty in the world around you. You'll be able to let go of your resentment and see things differently, which will help your relationships grow.

Archangel Jeremiel

This archangel is in charge of wisdom and understanding. He helps us find clarity in our lives by teaching us how to face our fears, overcome our obstacles, and deal with negativity. He's there to help us prepare for life's inevitable challenges and take them head-on.

Signs Archangel Jeremiel Is Present

You feel inspired and motivated to achieve your goals. This angel wants you to be clear on what you want out of life, and he'll help you take a step in the right direction to succeed in the end. He'll give you the courage you need and show you how to face everything head-on, either with a smile or crying because it was so hard.

You recognize your fears. You may find yourself dealing with fears or insecurities, but this angel will show you how to overcome them by facing your fears head-on.

You face your obstacles. This angel is here to help you deal with anything that may be standing in your way of reaching your goals. He'll inspire you to be brave when you're afraid and teach you how to rise above any obstacle that lies in the path of what you want.

Archangel Sandalphon

In charge of music, this angel helps us make music in our lives. He guides us to find the harmony that allows us to make beautiful music.

Signs Archangel Sandalphon Is Present

You learn how to play an instrument. If you haven't learned an instrument yet, this angel will show you how easy it can be to pick up one. He'll also teach you about the different types of music so that deciding on what instrument you want to learn will be easy.

You are inspired to create. This archangel is in charge of making music in your life - whether it's a song, art, or dance - he'll help you bring your creative side out with every project. You may be working on an art project or writing lyrics for a new song. This angel will help you bring it all together and make something beautiful or move out of it.

You feel like you can weather the storm. This archangel is here to guide you through any storm life throws. He'll help you find the positive in life's hardships so that you'll dance with them gracefully.

Archangel Seraphiel

This is the archangel of prayer and purification. He helps us cleanse the body and mind when they are negativity-filled.

Signs Archangel Seraphiel Is Present

You are feeling cleansed and purified. This angel is there to purify your body and mind so that you'll feel renewed and ready to face every day. He'll help you rid your body of impurities and teach you how to keep impurities out through a good diet, positive thinking, and regular prayers.

You are praying more. This angel is there to support your prayers. He wants you to find peace with your dreams and desires so that you can reach out to God and ask for what you need in life. He's there to remind you of the power of prayer and that a higher power is helping you achieve your goals.

You can use your abilities for the greater good. Seraphiel is the angel of prayer, so he's there to help you find a powerful prayer life. He'll teach you how to pray more passionately than ever, leading you to holiness. You may have already had a prayer life before, but things will change dramatically once this angel enters your presence.

You have more energy. This angel will help you feel like you have more energy throughout the day to make the most out of your time. He'll encourage you to get up and keep going, so that life will be more enjoyable for you.

You feel less stressed. When you're feeling overwhelmed or stressed, this archangel will guide you toward a peaceful state of mind where nothing feels overwhelming anymore.

You are more clear-headed. When negativity takes over your mind, it can be hard to focus on anything else.

Archangel Raziel

This is the archangel of secrets, knowledge, and wisdom. He helps us uncover the secrets that are hidden in our lives so that we can uncover our inner wisdom and find true happiness.

Signs Archangel Raziel Is Present

You are drawn to hidden treasures. This angel is in charge of finding the gifts that come from keeping your eyes and ears open. He will help you see things in new ways to look at your life with a different set of eyes. He will teach you how to uncover treasures and valuable knowledge that you wouldn't see otherwise, which can lead to personal growth and change for the better.

You gain inner strength. You may have moments when it feels like the walls are closing in on you, but this archangel will help pull back those walls and give you the strength to move forward, even through the hardest times.

You awaken your inner wisdom. This angel will inspire you to look deeper into yourself and find your inner truth. Your knowledge might be greater than you realize, but this angel will help you recognize what's within your own mind.

You feel more fulfilled. It can be hard to get back on track whenever we're not happy with ourselves or feel a lack of fulfillment in our lives. This angel will help you get out of whatever rut you've fallen into and inspire you to find more fulfillment in your life.

How to Call on Archangels to Help You

1. **Say a prayer to them.** If you've never called on an archangel before, say a short prayer to them and ask them to fill your life with their presence.
2. **Ask for help.** Tell them what you need, and ask them to guide you toward it.

3. **Visualize.** While you are praying or asking for help, visualize yourself in a peaceful place and see them coming to visit you there. Tell them all you want to, trust that they've heard you, and you will receive an answer soon.
4. **Feel their love.** While calling upon your angels, allow yourself to feel the wave of love they give into the world. It will lift your spirits as they enter your heart and soul.
5. **Be grateful.** Say a thank-you prayer, and be grateful for everything that is going on in your life.
6. **Believe.** Trust that they will help you and remind you of their power to guide you toward a better life because they do.

How to Show Archangels You Honor Them

1. **Thank them.** Thank them for the gifts that they've given you and the blessings bestowed upon your life.
2. **Ask to serve.** Ask these angels to guide you toward serving others and bringing joy into people's lives. They will help you every step, bringing more joy into your life.
3. **Give thanks.** Give thanks for all of their help because it is their gift to you.
4. **Respect their presence within your life.** Take a moment each day to contemplate the archangels' presence, all they've done for you, and the fact that they have never let you down.

Doing these things will not only show them you value them but will guarantee that it's easier for you to connect with them each time you need them and get even faster and more dramatic results from drawing on their energy in your life.

Chapter Ten: Other Guides and How to Find Them

There are other beings that you can communicate and work with besides the ones we've mentioned in this book so far. Among them are plants, mythical creatures, star beings, and so on. So, without further ado, let's discuss all the other kinds of spirit guides and explain how you can work with them.

Plants as Spirit Guides

Plants can also be spirit guides.
https://pixabay.com/images/id-1498985

Can a plant be your spirit guide? Many believe that plants are your first spirit guides. After all, it was in nature that humans grew and developed a connection with the world around them. The plants within nature can be seen as a form of spirit guide for everyone because they have a sense of awareness and can communicate with you.

Some plants can also be used in nature magic spells, and that's because they have their own spirit with their own deep knowledge and wisdom, which could benefit you immensely, both physically and spiritually. If you are looking for a plant spirit guide to communicate with, you can use any plant that you like or work with the ones that call to you specifically.

There's nothing weird about being spiritually guided by a plant. Just because it remains rooted to a spot doesn't mean it's not very alive and sentient. This is an ideology rooted in plant spirit shamanism. Shamans know that plants have power and can act as a connection between the physical and spiritual worlds.

Plant spirit shamanism was practiced by the ancients and continues to be practiced today. Often, you can work with plants to help you heal your mind and body. To connect with the plants as spirit guides, you must learn to listen to their call. That's right. Plants actually speak to us. You'll realize this if you learn to pay attention.

Zion's story: "*Here's how a plant spirit guide helped me reconcile with my family once more. I had spent most of my life as a loner because of a terrible incident in my family where I was falsely accused of something I didn't do and therefore ostracized. I couldn't look at them in the same way ever again, especially since I saw them as evil. I soon cut myself off from the family because there was no other way for me to deal with them.*

After years of being totally estranged from some members of my family, I thought they were still stuck in the same cycle of dysfunction, and it didn't matter what either of us did or said to change that. Sadly, some family members continued to do the same thing, and I hated them even more.

This is how I spent my life. Every day was filled with memories of pain. I couldn't get away from the pain of my past, but that changed when I chose to connect with a plant spirit guide, and I met her in my dream. Her name was Elsie. She showed me how to connect with the world around me in a way that no other person had ever done before.

Elsie was my first plant spirit guide because she brought me into a whole new arena of consciousness and spirituality that opened up a new way for me to see life itself. I discovered that I could see the world as a spiritual phenomenon and that I wasn't stuck in a cycle of pain. As I learned more about myself and began using different plants as spirit guides to heal my mind and body, my life began to change for the better.

It was at this time when I met Elsie, and things started to get better for me. She helped me realize that not all people on this planet are bad and that many of them came here with good intentions. In fact, they came here seeking opportunities because they believed they could improve their lives through knowledge. With time, she began to share insight about my family, and she showed me who the culprit was that had sown discord between them and me. She even showed me where to look for proof I could use to exonerate myself. After years of being cut off, I reached out with this proof, and everyone realized their mistake. We came together, reconciled our differences, and now I have a love for my family once more."

Working with Plant Spirit Guides

1. **Spend more time in nature:** Doing this will make it possible for you to hear the trees and other plants around you. Walk around nature to hear the plants calling to you, and they will. Be very clear about your intention, and you should find yourself a plant spirit friend in no time.

2. **Connect your consciousness with that of the plant.** You can do this by tuning your senses to pay attention to the various qualities contained within the plant, as well as the healing power it has. You can do this by mindfully observing the plant by gazing at it. As you look, allow your heart to fully open up to the plant. Feel nothing but love, and wait expectantly.

3. **Treat the plants lovingly.** You should have respect for the plants. When you do, they're more willing to work with you. So, ensure you revere them by leaving them undisturbed rather than picking at them unnecessarily. You can even say some loving, kind words to the plant to develop a

relationship with its spirit. When that relationship is thriving, you can ask it what you will, and it will gladly show up for you in the best way it can.

Mythological Creatures as Spirit Guides

Don't let the fact that these creatures come from "myths" and myths are supposedly not true stop you from seeking a connection to them. The fact that we have these stories means that the consciousnesses of these creatures are very real indeed. The mythologies surrounding creatures like the mermaid, centaur, gorgon, and others will reveal much about their characters, letting you know who would be the best creature to work with to get results.

Now let's talk about these trans-species, which are part human, part beast. Whether it's a sphinx, harpy, faun, Minotaur, or fairy, it doesn't matter who you choose to work with as long as their energy matches yours. How will you know? It will feel right, and your intuition will confirm that you should be working with the being. Let's take a look at some of these creatures.

The centaur is famous, with a man's head and torso and a horse's legs and flank. Centaurs are powerful. They are fierce guardians of the wild spirit and the land and provide stability wherever they go. Centaurs can be fierce if you provoke them, but they are also very compassionate. The centaur has the strength of a man with the wisdom of a horse.

The fairy is another famous creature that commonly appears in folklore. Fairies are incredibly playful beings that love being in nature, roaming the earth, and playing tricks on humans to make them happy. Fairies also have a natural connection with healing because their energies align well with nature and herbs, trees, flowers, and water. All fairies love music, for it brings out their natural creative energy.

The gorgons happen to be sisters from Greek mythology. Their names are Stheno, Euryale, and Medusa, the latter being the most popular of the bunch. The thing about them is that they were totally human - except for the fact that instead of hair, they had a mass of hissing snakes that writhed about on their heads. They were scary because to look upon them directly meant you'd be turned into stone in a heartbeat. Their energy can be very useful when you want to freeze an enemy who has been bugging you unnecessarily in their tracks.

The mandrake is a combination of humans and plants. It's also a set of plants you can find in the Mediterranean, and the interesting thing about them is that their roots resemble an actual face. Also, this plant is a known hallucinogen, which just adds to its lore. It's said that the plant has a scream so loud when it's dug up from the earth that anyone within earshot will die instantly. You may remember this from a certain popular movie franchise based on a series of magical books.

The mermaid is popular, with a woman's torso and head and a fish's lower body. This mythological creature has its roots in Assyria, from ancient times. It is said that Atargatis, the goddess, had been terribly ashamed because she was responsible for the death of her lover, who was human. To punish herself, she chose to turn herself into a mermaid. Since this time, many tales have been told about this creature, and some swear they have met them.

The selkie has Scottish and Irish roots, being half woman and half seal.

The Minotaur is half man, half bull, and etymologically, its name is based on Minos, a bull god of Crete, specifically the Minoans. Minos was also a king who demanded to be fed meals made by the youth of Athens.

The satyr is of Greek origin, and this creature is half man, half goat. The Roman version is known as the faun. It's relatively safe, except around women. This being is devoted to hedonism and wants nothing more than sheer pleasure, no matter how it gets it.

The siren is also from Greece mythology. Its torso and head are human, and it has a bird's tail and legs. This was not a creature sailors ever wanted to meet on their voyages because it most certainly meant doom, a gloomy, watery death for all who would hear her seductive tune lulling them onto dangerous reefs. Homer wrote an epic known as "The Odyssey," and here, when Odysseus was making his way back from Troy, he had to have himself tied securely to the ship's mast so that he wouldn't give in to the siren's melodies.

The sphinx has a human head and a lion's body. Sometimes, you'll see it depicted with an eagle's wings and a snake's tail. This is rooted in ancient Egyptian mythology on account of the Giza sphinx. It was also in Greek mythology. Each time it shows up in a story, danger comes. It will ask humans to answer tough questions, which, when not answered correctly, would cause it to devour them angrily. This was also a creature that played a role in Oedipus's story. Oedipus gave the Sphinx a correct answer, but he had to pay the price. The Greek myths hold that the head of a sphinx is a woman's, while the Egyptian ones insist it's a man.

Which Creature Should You Work With?

One thing you can do to figure things out is to think about the attributes of the animals that these creatures have as part of who they are. Would you like to channel the bravery and ruthlessness of a lion? Perhaps you should work with the sphinx. You should also consider what each creature is known for. Would you like to work some sweet magic where you're sweet in your methods but get deadly, effective results? The siren is a good pick. Want to find a way to forgive yourself for some wrong you did in the past? Then how about working with the mermaid? It's all down to you.

On the other hand, don't assume your choice has to make sense. You can pick one, work with it, and see the results you get. If you're not getting anything useful, try another. Eventually, you'll land upon what you should work with.

Another way to pick would be to choose the ones that resonate with your preferred gender or the ones that your ancestors thought were worth their time and effort. You could check in with your other guides to see what's right for you, use a pendulum as we've talked about in an earlier chapter, or ask that they reveal themselves to you as you go to bed at night.

Star Beings

These are other civilizations in the stars and not part of the human race. It is believed that among regular humans, some of us are star seeds, which means we incarnated here from one of the star systems to fulfill some mission on this Earth. Let's take a look at some of these beings in detail.

Pleiadians. Pleiadians are a group of collective consciousness extraterrestrial beings who have intervened in human events for the last twenty-five thousand years. They hail from the Pleiadian star system called Pleiades, one of the oldest in our galaxy, bearing seven planets called the Seven Sisters inhabited by their own kind and other life forms. They are here to assist humanity, who is living through a great transformation at this time.

We have had many experiences in which Pleiadians helped us and communicated with us, sometimes while we were awake and aware that they were present, while at other times while we were asleep, dreaming what seemed to be normal human dreams. Their civilizations have thrived for hundreds of thousands, if not millions, of years. They were likely the first to contact Earth at some point in antiquity, often humanoid in appearance and communicating by telepathy. They keep records on behalf of the earth, have advanced and rapid healing abilities, and are interested in all those who want to grow in consciousness.

Sirians: The Sirians are a collective of beings from the Sirius star system. The Sirians have coexisted with Earth and our Solar System for eons. There is evidence that the Sirian systems have been manipulated and seeded by a larger collective of beings who use the Draco and Orion star systems as their "farmland," so to speak. The entities who manage the Draco and Orion systems are typically (but not necessarily) reptilian in nature, while those in Sirius are humanoid.

Sirius is a star that is less than nine light-years from Earth, making it the second-closest star to us. It's the brightest star in the sky and the only one named after a living being, the Dog Star. Sirius has at least two giant planets believed to be about the size of Jupiter and possibly other planets. Like our Sun, Sirius has a companion star — a white dwarf called Sirius B (the "Pup"). This partner star revolves around Sirius relatively rapidly, completing an orbit in just 50 years. Sirians are the ones who keep the peace and guard the world, so it's safe for us all.

Arcturians: Arcturian aliens are a collective of beings from the Arcturus star system. They are sometimes collectively referred to as the Tall Whites by some. Arcturians have visited Earth occasionally but prefer to remain in the background where they can observe without interference.

The name "Arcturians" is also used to describe an intelligent species native to Arcturus's four gas giant planets. These planets were seeded with life by a race of Zeta Reticuli-type beings who arrived there from Sirius C in our solar system thousands of years ago. The Arcturian system is about 36.7 light-years from Earth and has a planet very similar to Earth. At this time, approximately 150 million beings are living in the Arcturian realm at any one time. They were among the very first races in our galaxy to achieve galactic travel, and they originated in a star system called Alpha Centauri, four light-years away from ours. These beings have a strong will, are natural leaders, and are the ones we can credit for building the world.

Andromedans: Andromedans are a collective consciousness extraterrestrial race living on and visiting Earth for at least thousands of years. They are one of the most advanced races in our galaxy and have been here to assist humanity, who is living through a great transformation at this time. They require highly evolved spiritually as well as technologically.

The Andromedan race originated in our own galaxy, where they advanced spiritually and technologically far beyond their ancestors. As revealed in some unidentified ancient texts, they arrived here at the same time that Earth's dinosaurs became extinct, roughly 65 million years ago, which alters the conventional explanation for the demise of those creatures (which is usually attributed to a meteor strike). They alone know what their purpose is, but they're great at accessing the akashic records, where everything that has ever happened or will ever happen is stored.

Orions: The Orion Alliance is a collective of beings from the Orion star system. They are sometimes collectively referred to as the Tall Whites by some. A maverick group of ancient civilizations, they think and act very differently from us. They often don't communicate to us in our own language but through symbols that we recognize but don't consciously think about. They do their best to protect Earth and humanity. Still, they can be a little too controlling at times, which is why they use negative manipulation on certain individuals or groups on Earth who have not yet learned how to free themselves from these influences. They want to improve our science and technology, and they want to help us see the potential we have.

Lemurians and Atlanteans: Lemuria and Atlantis were one and the same. Eventually, both cultures split into two groups: those who wanted to return to the past and those who wanted to bring in the new age. Those who wished to return to Lemuria created the Bermuda Triangle, a place to escape or draw energy. Atlanteans had better technology than our own, and they could bring a lot of energy to the planet. Atlantis was indeed an advanced society that thrived for thousands of years.

Lyrans: Lyrans are a collective of beings from the Lyran star system. They have coexisted with Earth and our Solar System for eons. The Lyran system has a planet very similar to Earth. At this time, several hundred thousand beings are living in the Lyran realm at any one time. They were among the very first races in our galaxy to achieve galactic travel, and they originated in a star system called Vega. We have to thank these beings for creating fire and humanity itself.

How to Contact These Spirit Guides

1. **Reach out to your guides by scrying.** Scrying involves gazing into a crystal or other reflective object and seeing images that can help you communicate with them. You can create a quick reflective surface by filling a dark bowl with water in a dark room, lighting a candle, and then staring into the water until things begin to reveal themselves. Don't force yourself to see what isn't there. Spend 15 minutes per session, and don't be upset if you see nothing the first few times. Something will come to you eventually.
2. **Make an altar.** If you want to contact your guides, make an altar where they can sit and reveal themselves to you. An easy way to do this is to create a small table with images of the beings you want to contact and a candle.
3. **Meditate.** Keep the essence of the being on your mind as you do so.
4. **Visualize.** See these beings in your mind's eye during your meditation.

5. **Try Bibliomancy.** This means using random passages from the Bible to glean information from these beings. You can simply open your Bible or any other book to a random page and read the first thing your eyes fall on. Note what that is because if the meaning isn't clear to you at first, it will be much later.

Conclusion

You've finally come to the end of this book, and it's been quite a trip. You now have all the information you need to begin communicating with your guides. Before wrapping this up, it's worth making it very clear that it's one thing to read about your guides and another thing entirely to develop a relationship with them. Just because you know it doesn't mean they'll show up automatically. You have to be the one to reach out and make it clear to them that you're ready and can develop something serious with them.

It should also be stated for the record that this is a matter of constant practice. In other words, just because something phenomenal hasn't happened since you began meditating or visualizing for a week or two doesn't mean you should quit. Think of this less as some quick fix to handle your life problems and more as a lifestyle. It's a great idea to pick a specific time of day or night to practice what you must connect with your guides. When you make a habit of it, it becomes a ritual, priming the pump so that you and your spirit guides can bridge the divide between you and begin to work together meaningfully.

Please be very wary about preparing and staying safe before performing any spiritual exercises. The last thing you want is to attract a mischievous spirit masquerading as the deity or being you want to connect with. So, take your time cleansing yourself. Clear the clutter in your mind and in your meditation space, too. Make sure your intention is very strong about who it is you want to reach out to, and you should be just fine.

While it's okay to ask your guides for things, please don't just reach out only when you need help. You should commune with them, honor them, and say hello, just because. Think about it. You don't like it when people only reach out when they need things, do you? Well, your guides aren't any different. You want to have a relationship with them, not just transactions. They began to bless me beyond my wildest dreams when I became intentional about connecting with them and honoring them without expecting anything in return. Sometimes they're the ones reaching out to me. Now that's the sort of relationship worth having with beings that know more than you and love you more than anyone else could. I wish you good luck on your spiritual journey. Have fun getting to know your guides.

Part 2: Archangels

Unlocking Secrets of Working with an Archangel, Spirit Guides, and Guardian Angels

Introduction

Getting a basic understanding of what angels are is the key to a deeper, more meaningful spiritual life for anyone remotely interested in their existence. If you want to learn more about angels, then you'll enjoy this book. It is ideal for anyone who has a basic understanding of the Bible but is also an easy-to-read entry point for those who do not know much (or anything) about angels.

The Bible contains a substantial amount of information about angels, but there are many other books on the topic by authors who claim to have insider knowledge on angels. They claim to have access to the spirit realm, allowing them to reveal secrets people are not supposed to know. However, these secret insights are often nothing more than conjecture mixed with ancient superstitions. The information in this book is different as it is based on what scholars and historians agree can be verified as facts.

The truth is that angels exist, clearly and undeniably, and the strongest reason for believing that they exist in the first place is because of the miraculous stories that people have written and told about them, not to mention the substantial amount of evidence that skeptics cannot easily explain away. This book is meant to answer many questions you may have thought about – but never had the chance to explore fully.

This is not just a book but an opportunity to change your life by moving into a new way of thinking about angels. Armed with this book, you'll have the knowledge and credibility to openly discuss what you have learned about the archangels in your life. You can accurately explain who they are and why they are important in your life. Most importantly, you can be sure that your thoughts and beliefs are based on fact, not myth, not conjecture, but fact. If you are ready to move from being a curious onlooker of the subject of angels to a knowledgeable believer, then this book will be an invaluable resource in your journey. Let's get right into it.

Chapter One: Angels and Archangels 101

Angels are beings who exist in many cultures, religions, and beliefs. Some believe they are spirits of deceased people, while others believe they are simply symbols of grace. They are typically described as beautiful human-like beings with radiant skin and wings who descend to Earth to bestow their grace upon mortals. The word angel comes from the Latin word *angelus,* meaning "messenger." The oldest myths of angels date back to the Mesopotamian and East Asian cultures. These cultures created mythical beings to interpret the world and guide humans. These myths involved angels who carried prayers from Earth to heaven and the gods who relied on them for messages sent by humans to the heavens. The belief in angels became more widespread during the Jewish exile to Babylon when priests and scribes began interpreting the Mesopotamian stories and incorporating them into their religion.

Although the idea of a god on high came from Mesopotamian culture, Christians began to believe that God's heavenly hosts did not simply serve as messengers between humans and heaven. Instead, God created them as a way for humans to know that heaven existed. They were believed to appear in dreams and visions, considered holy messages by the people who had them. However, they were also believed to interact with humans once they began to fall out of favor with their Heavenly Father. Turning away from God would result in an angel becoming demonic and manipulative.

Islam offers an interpretation of angels that is very similar to Christian angelology. Angels are considered divine beings created by Allah who carry out His will on Earth. Muslim angels are also called angels, although Islam does not believe in heaven. They are believed to embody God's knowledge and power and have no physical bodies. However, their influence is not restricted to the afterlife. Many Muslims believe angels are found worldwide, acting as divine agents to those who deserve them.

Although angels are believed to carry out God's will and act on his behalf, Christianity views angels as having a more protective role. They are not merely messengers between humans and heaven but also serve to protect people from evil forces. In Christianity, they are often called guardian angels and are believed to be assigned to everyone at birth. Unlike Islam and Judaism, Christianity teaches that angels have a physical body, although they do not eat, drink, or experience any physical pleasure. Furthermore, the Christian belief is that angels are the only beings that God created before the creation of humans. They are considered to be immortal, divine, and timeless.

Judaism does not subscribe to the concept of guardian angels. However, it does believe in angels who watch over and protect people at all times. The Jewish laws that govern every aspect of a person's life require angels as messengers and intermediaries between man and God. Angels are believed to be bound by God's commandments and do not stray from them. They have no free will nor desire because they serve as extensions of God's will in relation to humans.

The Hindu religion considers angels as beings who exist in the natural world and provide guidance to humans. Angels in Hinduism are considered to be highly evolved spirits who have existed since the creation of the universe but never incarnated as physical beings. They are believed to possess multiple aspects that can be altered at any time. For example, if humans commit a sin like greed, then the angelic forms of greed will appear on Earth while those aspects of goodness remain unaffected.

Zoroastrianism believes in a good and evil god and in the existence of angels, although they are not believed to be divine beings. In fact, Zoroastrians believe that there are three separate groups of angels:

- Amesha Spentas, who govern goodness
- Yazatas, who govern the elements
- Daevas, who are described as evil spirits

Although each group represents one particular characteristic, Zoroastrians believe the world is made up of malevolent and benevolent forces. This world is represented by the struggle between these two forces, which are always in conflict. Zoroastrianism does not believe that angels have individual wings, nor do they carry out God's will. Interestingly enough, the Yazatas are thought to inhabit the bodies of humans who were once followers of Zarathustra, the prophet of Zoroastrianism. This taught that by becoming a follower of Zoroaster, followers would become divine themselves.

Buddhism does not support the concept of angels but does encourage belief in spirits. These spirits exist in two separate areas, the heavens and the Earth. Unlike angels, who are considered to be divine beings with no physical form, Buddhist spirits are embodied by humans who have died. A bodhisattva is believed to be a being whose soul has reincarnated into a celestial or earthly form so that it can achieve enlightenment and assist humans on Earth.

The Japanese religion of Shinto is based on a belief in angels. In fact, the Japanese belief holds that the practice of having a shrine at one's home has been passed down from ancient times and was first performed by an angel. The concept of angels in various religions has evolved over time and taken many forms of development, geography, and culture. However, there are some common elements found in each religion. Guardian angels protect their human charges, humans who will one day become angels themselves, physical bodies that allow them to interact with humans, and the interaction between good and evil forces on Earth.

The Angelic Hierarchy

The concept of heaven is a powerful one that has captured the interest and imagination of people for thousands of years. After all, who does not want to believe that the beings who are from such a phenomenal place can look out for us on Earth? However, it raises the question of whether all angels are equal in rank and power. The answer seems to be no. Why is this? The answer lies in the writings in the Bible, which speak of a hierarchy of angels between heaven and Earth.

In 1513 AD, a German monk named Fra Luca Gauricus published a book titled Dialogues on the Life of Jesus Christ. It was first printed in Latin and later reprinted in several European languages such as French, German, Italian, and Spanish. In this book, Gauricus included an allegorical painting depicting the story of how an angel tempted Adam and Eve to eat from the tree of knowledge of good and evil. There were two angels depicted in this work, one who tempted Eve and another who came to her rescue (or intervened).

These two angels, who represent a very different sort of angelic being from everything else we have mentioned so far, are considered to be one of Christianity's most important and unique angels. The detail in Fra Luca's painting depicts them as having six wings and no legs. They are described as being dressed all in white with flowing hair and a crown or as a tall man with a long robe. This depiction has stuck to this day and is used by some Christian churches in their artwork.

Some people may be aware of the angelic hierarchy but may not understand how it operates. The hierarchy has to do with the work of the angels. The most famous angel is Michael, but many others above and beneath him carry out different tasks. It is all part of their role as agents of God's will in the world, which is to help humans accomplish their purpose on Earth. This hierarchy is divided into nine ranks known as choirs, and each possesses distinct characteristics identified by their particular level in the hierarchy.

The Seraphim

The highest rank in the angelic hierarchy is that of the Seraphim. They are considered to be the closest angels to God and therefore receive his love and light. They are considered to be the guardians of the throne of God. Traditionally, they have six wings and two sets of eyes. The first set is in the front, where there are two eyes known as "the eyes of love," and the second set is on top, which can see everything at all times. Above their heads is a halo or ring like a rainbow that shines with light like a thousand suns combined into one great brilliance. The Seraphim are also said to have feet of gold and hands like crystals. In the Old Testament of the Bible, there is a reference to seraphim residing in the Temple of Solomon. They were said to be the angels who guarded the Ark of the Covenant and served God. There is evidence that people worldwide worshiped seraphim in ancient times, including in India, China, Japan, and many other places across Europe.

The Cherubim

The next highest rank after the Seraphim is that of the Cherubim. The Cherubim are described as having four faces and four wings. They are also said to have two arms and a breastplate embellished with precious stones. The cherubim appear to be the same as the seraphim but have just two pairs of wings and one pair of arms. The Cherubim are known as protectors who guard God's throne in heaven. They are also said to be the guardians of God's will on Earth. In fact, they are even mentioned in the Old Testament concerning Adam and Eve. When they left their Garden home, they were stationed outside Eden with a flaming sword to guard the path to the tree of life. The Cherubim are a symbol of innocence and purity, and because of this, many people like to put them in their artwork or religious homes so that they can connect with these qualities within themselves.

The Thrones

The next rank after the Cherubim is that of the Thrones. They are said to be a flaming wheel with a thousand eyes, and God sits in the center of this wheel. It is believed that this is the same wheel described in the book of Ezekiel. It states, *"Above it (the throne) were the wheels of fire, and all four wheels had the same likeness. The appearance of the wheels was like a wheel in the middle of a wheel"*. These wheels have eyes made of fire, and they are not just there to be decorative but to represent the presence of God and his will on Earth. They stay nearest to God and remain in his presence always.

The Dominions

This rank of angels are the keepers of divine order, think middle administration. They are in charge of the universe's rules, laws, and regulations and hence are concerned with ensuring that all humans follow these laws. They also oversee all human activity, which is why they can be considered a task force investigating social misconduct. This order of angels is also known as Hashmallim and is seen as responsible for earthquakes, storms, and other natural disasters. However, it is implied that they get these orders from God, who sends them to do his will. The leader of this group is the angel of mercy, Zadkiel.

The Virtues

With a form like orbs of light, these angels are charged with the maintenance of nature. Throughout history, the Virtues have been known as healers and can be thought of as responsible for ensuring that nature functions optimally. They bestow miracles upon those who deserve it, as instructed by the higher-ranking angels. In the Bible, it was said that these angels were present when Jesus ascended into heaven.

The Powers

The Powers are variously described as a floating mass or cloud of fire or possessing the form of a winged bull. They are the closest ranks to humanity and, thus, have certain charges related to human affairs. They look over justice in society by ensuring everyone understands what laws and rules apply to them. They are responsible for the welfare of humanity and are often charged with teaching. However, like humans, they are vulnerable to acts of sin and can become immoral.

The Principalities

This rank of angels is often depicted in art as light rays. They are thought to be in charge of the individual nations of the Earth and religious groups, but they also have a responsibility for all humanity. They are in charge of all situations involving law, science, and technology. They also govern the activities of the regular angels below them and ensure that everyone carries out their tasks properly.

Archangels and Angels

Archangels are the highest rank of angels. Their job is to help people and bring them closer to God by guiding them on their path through life and sometimes giving them messages from him. They have been known since the earliest times as presences who watch over specific affairs of man. The word archangel comes from the Greek *arkhangelos* meaning "the chief angel."

In practice, there are only four archangels: Michael, Gabriel, Raphael, and Uriel. However, Enoch's book mentions an extra three, Remiel, Saraquael, and Raguel. The name Michael is derived from a Hebrew word meaning, "He who is like God." The name Gabriel means "the strength of God," Raphael means "God's healing," and Uriel means "light of God" while also having a reference to being in the presence of God.

Pre-Christian views on archangels vary significantly from those held today. For example, in early Christian thought, the archangels Michael and Gabriel were thought to function as bringers of guidance and revelation, while Raphael was considered more of an aesthetic figure. Today, most modern theologians regard Michael as the leader of the other archangels and Gabriel as the sole angel who appeared to Mary in the New Testament.

Michael the Archangel, also known as the Ancient of Days, watches over all of humanity. He is the chief angel in charge of all matters concerning mankind. Although many Christians see him as ruling the angels, he does not do this directly. Rather, he is the leader of all archangels because he is said to be among the oldest angels in existence. In some legends, he appears to humanity members with unique qualities and needs and often grants special powers to those who need them most. Michael was said to be present when Jesus ascended into heaven and is often painted in Christian art as wearing scale mail armor that covers his legs and feet, with his armor being decorated by various small stars or crosses.

Gabriel the Archangel is seen as the messenger of God. He is said to be the one who brings messages to man from God and gives guidance to those who want it. In the New Testament book of Revelation, he is given a central role in bringing news of the story of

Jesus Christ's return to earth and his final victory over Satan. When Jesus was taken up into heaven, it was Gabriel that brought this news down to Mary, his mother.

Raphael the Archangel is seen as a healing angel and will visit sick people in their dreams with messages from God if they require healing. He is often depicted as wearing red robes and having wings, signifying his role as healer and guide.

Uriel the Archangel is seen as the angel of wisdom and repentance. He is said to be the cherub tasked with guarding the gate of Eden. He is also the angel of death that swept across Egypt on the Passover and the angel sent to warn Noah about the flood.

Archangels have appeared in various religions across the world. In Islam, the Archangel Gabriel appeared to Muhammad and revealed the Qur'an to him. In Judaism, Gabriel is the angel of death. In Christianity, he appeared to Mary and informed her of the birth of Jesus. Gabriel is also believed to be the angel who will sound the trumpet on the last day, but this is a Christian belief because the Muslims believe it is the Archangel Raphael who will perform this action.

The term "archangel" is also used in the Zoroastrian tradition. Of the seven Holy Immortals, two are archangels, Mithra and Rashnu. Here, they serve as intermediaries between God and man. In Wicca, archangels are often called "guardians" or "elemental kings." They have been reinterpreted as identical to other authoritarian deities from other religions, such as Jehovah and Satan, although most adherents acknowledge them as separate beings.

Archangels have been depicted in many styles and types of clothing. In Christian art, Michael is often shown wearing a winged helmet and is often carrying a flaming sword. Gabriel is commonly seen as wearing a light-blue tunic and has wings, which is his usual appearance in the book of Revelation. Raphael was believed to wear the same clothing as Michael but with a red cape or robe. Uriel has been portrayed with armor like that of Michael but without the wings. However, Uriel can also be seen as having black robes and usually has a spear in his right hand, which references his role as an angel of death.

Archangels have been depicted in religious art for several centuries, with early examples of archangel art dating back to at least the 1st century. The oldest surviving representation of an angel is from the 10th-century "Book of Durrow." The painting depicts a winged figure with a halo sitting on top of a tree trunk, which symbolizes death. In some depictions, this image is accompanied by another figure with outstretched wings and a halo. This second being has been interpreted as an angelic demon who takes control of the first and represents death. Later Christian art views Michael as the most important archangel, and he often appears in paintings or sculptures holding his flaming sword. In this way, he can be compared to the Hindu god Shiva, who protects the world with a divine sword. An early depiction of Raphael is by the Italian Renaissance artist Giovanni Lanfranco who painted him with a scallop shell in his right hand. The scallop shell as a symbol is related to immortality since some believe that if – upon death – one has a scallop shell in their hand, they will become immortal.

In Occultism, Uriel has been viewed as a key spiritual force that can remove negative or evil spirits. Many modern-day occultists, however, believe that Uriel should be seen as the archangel who controls the forces of nature, while Gabriel controls the four elements, fire, earth, wind, and water. As well as this, they believe that Michael should be seen as being in charge of spiritual energies and all good things in life, while Raphael is in charge of healing and love. While this view may be popular among some occultists, it is not a view shared by many known mainstream religions.

The difference between Archangels and regular angels is an aspect of the archangel's role in the Judeo-Christian tradition. In the Bible, God sends regular angels to carry out his will, but the archangels are special angels who are given higher status and are more potent than other regular angels. The two most prominent archangels, Michael and Gabriel, were sent by God to carry out crucial tasks that affected all of humanity. Michael had a major role in defeating Satan and leading humanity to salvation, while Gabriel had a major role in revealing messages and prophecies from God to humans.

The Christian and modern-day Jewish beliefs in archangels are largely derived from their belief in angels and the angelic hierarchy.

In Christian belief, angels have been seen as the messengers of God. Because of this, they are believed to have a hierarchical system of ranks. However, some Protestant churches do not agree with these hierarchies and do not believe that there is a hierarchy of angels. The Catholic Church believes that *there is* – but does not believe that these hierarchies are as strict or structured as they were in the past.

Frequently Asked Questions

Q: How many angels are there?

A: Scholars estimate anywhere from millions to billions of angels. Most, however, agree that there are at least several million.

Q: What does an angel look like?

A: There are many descriptions of angels and what they look like. In the Old Testament, they are described as winged creatures, and in the New Testament, they have human-like features and have been said to have wings and halos. Other descriptions say angels are tall with big muscles and radiant hair or skin. In other ancient texts, angels are described as being made entirely of light.

Q: Do Archangels have personalities?

A: Throughout most of the Bible, archangels are not given human-like personalities. However, in many modern religions, such as Judaism and Christianity, archangels are portrayed as being intelligent and having individuality.

Q: Do all religions have Archangels?

A: In fact, not all religions have archangels. Some religions, such as the Hindu religion and certain Native American religions, do not believe in archangels at all. Other religions, however, believe in archangels and call them different names.

Q: Do angels have a gender?

A: Angels are believed to be genderless. The genderless nature of angels is often debated. However, some religions believe that although angels have no gender, they still identify with a specific gender.

Q: Can I really connect to an angel or Archangel?

A: Connecting to an angel or Archangel is possible and has been done by people throughout history. A noteworthy example is the clairvoyant mystic Edgar Cayce, who was able to connect to Archangel Michael and receive detailed information about his role and the role of other angels.

There are many things to consider when thinking about angels and archangels. For example, every religion has its own interpretation of what an angel or Archangel is and how they should act or appear. Some religions believe that angels are winged creatures, while others believe that they are genderless beings. A few religions believe that angels are completely made of light and have no solid form. These opposing beliefs make it hard for people who practice different religions to agree on the identity of an angel or Archangel. However, many religions do not dismiss the role angels and Archangels play in the world. Almost all religions believe that angels have a significant role in life and can be used to help humans with their daily struggles and quests for knowledge. So, if you have ever wondered what an angel or Archangel is and their role, you may feel more comfortable knowing that in almost all religions, they are treated as pure beings whose sole purpose is to help humans.

Chapter Two: Spirit Guides Basics

Spirit guides are the unseen allies of your spiritual journey to help provide wisdom and insight. They exist to offer guidance and support through every step of life. Spiritual guides are not a religious idea but rather an ancient universal concept that can be found in many cultures across the globe. The guides may come in many forms, including animal familiars, angels, nature spirits, and even loved ones around you. They may be present in the physical world, the astral plane, or the dimension.

Guides can even be part of your higher self or a spirit form on another level entirely. They may appear and disappear, speak to us through our dreams, or come in a rush of energy and emotion. They can help us to heal emotionally, mentally, and physically. Sometimes they can even perform acts of magic for us as well. Though some can be messengers of healing, protection, love, and enlightenment, they are messengers of warning. Spirit guides serve as our guardians in the astral world, the plane we go to when we sleep or go into altered states of consciousness through meditation or shamanic work.

In ancient times, spirits were thought to inhabit every stone, tree, and body of water. Today, however, with science advancing rapidly, we are more aware that all things on the physical plane have a spiritual dimension. Ancient cultures believed that everything was made up of energy, not just the physical world but even our beings. The human body is made up of energy, and human beings themselves are also made up of energy.

Spirit guides are a part of this same energy, but on a higher level than we are. In other words, they are an integral part of our being that resides in many dimensions simultaneously, both in the physical plane and beyond. They are the fuel that keeps our spiritual journey running. Through them, we can gain access to a greater sense of self-awareness and information on how to deal with life's challenges. When we work with spirit guides, they can give us advice far more helpful than what we receive from friends or family members.

Throughout human history, people have felt that they were guided through life by unseen forces. They felt that their lives and destinies were planned out in advance and that there was a reason for everything that happened to them. This idea is expressed throughout many world religions, especially those from Asia and Europe, as well as Native American culture. It is a very comforting idea for many people because it explains things we do not understand about our existence here on Earth. Many of us yearn to have a deeper connection with our higher selves and the universe; spirit guides may be the missing link.

Spirit Guides in Native America

In Native American culture, the belief in spirit guides is very strong. When a child is born, a ceremony is performed in which the parents give the child a name for both their human and spiritual selves. Sometimes this is also done for an adult who may need to be reconnected with their spirit guides. A shaman, or medicine person, will be called to perform the ceremony.

Native American cultures believe that every individual has at least one primary spirit guide who is always there for us in our day-to-day lives. This can be an animal or other forms of nature, such as wind or water. These are usually quiet spirits who do not make themselves known unless someone is in danger or needs assistance. They are there to help us in our times of need but will always remain hidden from us unless we specifically call upon them. These are the spirits who guide us through major life events. They will watch over us throughout our entire lives as we go through significant transitions and make big decisions. These guides work with other spirits to help provide guidance for each person's highest good. They are likely to appear at times of transition, helping guide people into a new direction or path. At other times, they may be seen during particularly difficult or upsetting moments, offering comfort and support to those who need it most.

Spirit Guides in the Bible

The Bible mentions spirit guides many times throughout ancient texts and scriptures. These passages tell of many spirits who watch over people throughout their lives, helping to guide and protect them. One of the spirit guides mentioned in the Bible is Gabriel, the archangel. In the book of Luke, he helps guide Mary through the birth of Jesus Christ. He assists her with protection and wisdom at a time when she has to make a very important decision about how to proceed with her pregnancy. Gabriel, who plays a central role in the story of Mary and Jesus, is an important spirit guide for many people because it is said that he comes to us through the Virgin Mary. The second time we hear of Gabriel is in the book of Daniel. He plays an important role in Daniel's life, protecting him from harm during the times of his greatest suffering and decision-making. This protection enabled him to fulfill his mission as God's chosen prophet. We learn that Gabriel has a special flair for ensuring those in need are protected and can do what they came here to do. This is why he is sometimes called the guardian.

The Book of Job tells us about another important spirit guide. Interestingly, this spirit guide is not one that anyone can see or hear as it is invisible and intangible, but we can feel its presence as it fills our days with comfort, peace, and protection. To say that this spirit guided Job would be an understatement because it is said that it protected him from all harm by traveling in whirlwinds at his side.

Spirit Guides and Shamanism

Much like Native Americans, shamanic cultures also believe in spirit guides and other spiritual beings who watch over each individual and help them throughout their lives. A shaman is someone who is called upon to help people through the use of spirit guides. They will meditate with them, pray to them, and commune with them in special ceremonies. These ceremonies are usually performed alone, but they can also be performed in groups under the watchful guidance of the shaman. During these special ceremonies, the shamanic practitioner seeks to contact their spirit guides with them. They do this through meditation and by making offerings and performing sacred dances. Shamanic practitioners believe that it takes a great deal of discipline to find your spirit guides and work with them personally. It also requires a great deal of trust in both the spiritual guides themselves and in the process of uncovering their true nature.

African Spirit Guides

African cultures believe strongly in the concept of spirit guides. Many African cultures have a spiritual leader who is known to have special connections to the spirits and knowledge of what is to come in the future. These spiritual leaders make their home with their people and are called their "spirit brothers." They tend to be very humble and respected and often do the exact opposite of what society expects them to do. They will spend most of their time in seclusion, out of sight, but are always with the people who they serve. They watch over these people and protect them from harm, sickness, or poverty.

In many African tribes, a person is born with a particular spirit guide who will remain with them throughout their lives. These guides help them see clearly and live a long, fulfilled life free of disease and other strife. In other traditions, the spiritual guide comes to people during times of transition in life. It may come at birth, death, or a major decision, such as an engagement or marriage. Some popular spirit guides in Africa are the Orishas, the gods and goddesses of the Yoruba religion. Despite originating in West Africa, these deities are also venerated in Brazil, Cuba, Haiti, and other Caribbean countries. The Orishas are called upon to help people and answer their questions during difficult times, including death and loss. Well-known Orishas are:

- Sango (pronounced *"shahn-goh"* with an emphasis on the second syllable), the god of lightning and thunder
- Ogun, the god of war

- Osun, the goddess of love and femininity (pronounced "*Aw-shoon*" with an emphasis on the second syllable)
- Obatala, the creator
- Esu, the trickster (pronounced "*ay-shoo*")

In the Rastafarian faith, the concept of a spirit guide is emphasized in their beliefs about Haile Selassie I. In the early 20th century, Haile Selassie was viewed as an incarnation of God who was sent to lead his people in Africa. Many Rastafarians believed that he would return physically to Earth after his death in 1975. Death is not considered an end but a beginning within this belief system. Therefore, they believe that Haile Selassie is still alive and has left his body to live among them on Earth as their spirit guide.

In Haiti, spirit guides can be found in almost all aspects of Haitian culture. It is believed that spirits play a large role in society and that everyone has at least one spirit guide accompanying them throughout life. Haitian spirit guide beliefs include everything from the ancestors that live in the forest to the spirits of plants and animals. In some parts of Haiti, religious leaders are believed to be spirit guides. These healers will use their powers to cure the ill or to bring prosperity or love into the lives of their people.

In African culture, spirit guides are believed to be able to communicate with the deceased and also hold power over the planet. They can be contacted through praying, dancing, or using sacred objects. African faith healers will often ask their gods and spirit guides for guidance when they perform a healing ceremony or divination. In these ceremonies, spiritual healers believe they can make contact with their spirit guides to gain insight or advice that they can use to help their patients.

Spirit Guides in Western Spiritualism

In Western Spiritualism and Occultism, spirit guides are very common. These spirit guides are believed to be invisible beings who can help people with their problems or advise them on what they should do in certain situations. Spirit guides can even allow people to reach out to them and talk with them by using an Ouija board or some kind of object which allows the guide to communicate on its own.

This concept of a spirit guide is similar to that of the shamanic practitioner but is not as commonly used in Western society because it is often viewed as a belief in magic or witchcraft. However, it is important to note that spirit guides are not exactly the same as spirit beings, such as ghosts or demons. Many cultures worldwide believe that spirits can be contacted through special rituals and ceremonies and are not necessarily evil or malevolent as they are perceived in Western mainstream religions.

Spirit Guides and the New Age Movement

The New Age Movement teaches that some gods and goddesses live on our planet and that they can teach us how to achieve spiritual enlightenment. To learn about these gods and goddesses and to ask them for advice or help, we must first recognize their presence in our lives and connect with them through meditation. Spirit guides can be contacted by many people, whether they are believers or not, in the New Age movement. This is because the practice of contacting spirit guides has become very popular today, especially among those who practice energy medicine. Some energy medicine practitioners believe that when you contact your spirit guides, you can use their power to heal yourself. By doing this, it is believed that you'll then be able to reach out to other people who may also need your healing power or advice.

Types of Spirit Guides

Spirit guides are often called upon to get advice or guidance on various matters or problems that someone may have. After all, these spirits can have great knowledge, wisdom, and understanding of the world around them. Your spirit guide is there for you to do just about anything you want them to do. They are there for you when you need to know what to do in certain situations, such as when you need help with a problem, advice on how to deal with certain people, or even when you need someone to cheer you on during difficult times in life. Your spirit guide does not judge you. They are there for you whether you are a good person or a bad person and whether you believe in a higher power or not.

Spirit guides can come into your life at any time. However, they will usually make their presence known when you need them the most, when you have a problem, or when something major happens in your life, such as moving to a new location or getting married. They can be people who have died and who still exist in our world as benevolent spirits; however, they can also be other entities like angels or animals. The following are some common spirit guides:

Spirit Animals: Many people believe spirit animals to be spirit guides, especially those who practice Paganism and Wicca. Many Pagans believe that each person has a sacred animal spirit that is familiar, who can help them perform spells and rituals. They say that you can create a bond with this animal through meditation when you are communicating with God or the Creator. The familiar is said to be able to protect its master from harm, especially if the two are paired together during rituals and spell casting. Within Native American society, the relationship between a magician and his familiar is like that of a dog and his master. A person's familiar will remain close to its master at all times, even when it has passed on into the afterlife. Types of animal familiars include snakes, cats, dogs, birds, etc. However, black cats are considered the most powerful animal familiars due to their ability to cause good and bad luck, depending on the situation.

Ancestors: In some cultures, the spirits of dead relatives are believed to be spirit guides. This is one of the most common types of spirit guides among African American spiritual healers and other cultural groups who practice religious ceremonies based on their dead ancestors. The spirits of the dead ancestors can be there to help you with your problems or to teach you how to live a better life. The spirits of your ancestors will also be able to teach you about their different personalities and how to learn from them and appreciate your unique life experiences.

Angels: Angels are believed to be the messengers of God and often work with other spirits to help people in need. They are known to be able to show you visions of the future, advise you on important matters, and help you with your problems. Whenever you feel like angels or spirit guides are around, there is usually a reason for it. Perhaps they are there to help you in your time of need, or maybe it is just part of their mission to watch over and protect you.

Ascended Masters: An ascended master is someone who has died and comes back to teach others about God or a higher power. These people have supposedly achieved higher spiritual enlightenment and are thus here to help you. They will be able to give you advice on how to live your life, achieve happiness, and avoid trouble in your life. The ascended masters are often the spirits of religious figures such as Jesus Christ, Buddha, Mary Magdalene, Confucius, and even the prophet Mohammed.

Elementals: Elementals are believed to be spirit guides and are also known as fairies, elves, or pixies. They are often associated with trees, water, and air and are sometimes thought of as nature spirits. They may appear in human form and can accompany specific humans throughout their lives. The elemental is believed to be able to create minor changes in nature that may include rain showers to help with drought conditions or make the sun shine brighter. They can also grant wishes, especially those involving love and luck.

Elementals are often associated with nature.
https://unsplash.com/photos/1EYMue_AwDw?utm_source=unsplash&utm_medium=referral&utm_content=creditShareLink

Higher Self: The higher self is also called the indwelling spirit, the true self, and is believed to be within one's mind or heart. It is said to have existed before birth and is within everyone. The higher-self guides a person through life, protects them, and helps them make decisions that are in their best interest. It also is said to be able to tell you what your purpose in life is and what your special talents are, and it may even give you the ability to see into your future.

People who have had Out-of-Body Experiences (OBEs) often report encountering spirit guides during their experience. Sometimes, these beings can give them advice or show them visions. Some people may also report contacting spirit guides while they are in a death-like state. During the time after death, a person may meet their spirit guides, who will provide guidance and assistance to help them through the transition period between death and the afterlife. At other times, spirit guides are said by those who claim to have OBEs to be manifestations of their higher mind. In this case, a person may make contact with their own Higher Self or their soul that has become separated from their physical body and is still wandering through the universe.

Why Should I Get in Contact with My Spirit Guide?

The term "spiritual" means something related to our consciousness or our soul. It can also refer to a divine entity or an unseen presence that we cannot explain with science and logic. In today's society, there is a great need to understand the importance of spirit guides in human life. Spirit guides can help you realize who you really are and your place in the universe. They can give you a glimpse of your true purpose in life and how you can easily fulfill it. If you let them, they will guide you through every aspect of your life, including your spiritual, emotional, and intellectual side. Spirit guides will always help you reach your full potential even if you think you know what is best for you. They will take you beyond the limits that were placed on you by genetics or bad experiences. When you understand and accept their role in your life, they will better guide you toward a greater understanding of God and the meaning behind all things.

Every person has a spirit guide. Learning how to communicate with this guide is important because you can ask them any question, and they will answer you. They will provide insight into your soul and help you find closure with past experiences. Spirit guides can help us in many ways, including manifesting our desires through their connection with the universe and helping us grasp the true meaning of our life experiences.

Real-life Accounts of Spirit Guides

Spirit guides have been witnessed and recorded in real-life experiences. Here are some brief examples:

- In 1975, a woman named Helen Smith claimed to have been in contact with her spirit guide, who she called Sophia, for 12 years. During this time, Sophia guided Helen through many issues that pertained to her life. She also helped to banish the spirits of those who were trying to do harm to her and her children in their home.

- Another woman named Sheila Wyatt claims that at the age of 14, she met a spirit guide who appeared in the form of a cat. This cat taught Sheila how to travel between parallel dimensions during astral projection and also how to heal using divine energies. Sheila uses this ability with her clients today by helping them heal illnesses through spiritual practices and energy work.

- A third-hand account existed in the book entitled "The World beyond Death: An Investigation of over 50 Near-Death and Other Experiences" by Dr. Raymond Moody. In this book, a man tells the story of how he was trapped in a well as a young boy. While trapped, he heard his spirit guide calling to him from above the well. The spirit said it was waiting for him to be rescued from the well and told him not to worry. The boy's father then found him and removed him from the well.

Although there is no scientific explanation for spirit guides, it is believed that we all have a spiritual element inside of us. We may never know why we are here, but there are things in life you already know about yourself that you did not pick up from your parents or other influences. Spirit guides can help us find these things about ourselves and teach us to be able to use them in our lives. They can also teach us about the universe and nature.

If you have never had an experience with your spirit guide, do not fret. Some people have never experienced the presence of their spirit guides either. Still, nearly everyone can experience its power and strength in their lives if they open themselves to its influence. The truth is, when you finally meet your guide, you will surely know it.

Chapter Three: Angelic Signs

Many people feel that angels are always there, giving us guidance and support. Whether we can see them or not, they always try to get through with messages for our benefit. What if you miss those signs because you did not know what they were trying to tell you? Understanding the signs is a great way to bridge the gap between angelic beings and humans. The most common signs include:

Noticing Their Presence

Do you ever feel as if someone is watching you when you are alone? While it is always nice to know that we are not completely alone in the world, this can sometimes be a little unsettling. This feeling is especially strong if someone seems to be following you around. According to ancient texts and lore, this is one of the most basic ways that angels tell us they are trying to send us messages. They will make their presence very noticeable if they want our attention until we get the memo. The contact can take any form, from soft tapping on your shoulder to a sudden chill in the air or even a sensation of someone walking up behind you. This physical contact can also be very subtle. Sometimes we can feel someone standing right behind us, almost touching our shoulders when we are, in fact, alone. The key is to look for these signs because they could be trying to get your attention.

Olfactory Sensations

When we think of angels, we think of them as very pure and divine beings. Since they are beyond time and space, there is no way of knowing that they are not constantly sending us smells that remind us of the purest things we have ever encountered. Whether it is the smell of flowers or a particular aroma that reminds you of your favorite childhood memory, this is a way that angels can get your attention. If you are having trouble understanding what your angels are trying to tell you, one of the best methods is to pay attention to what smells you are drawn to and the feelings they evoke in you. Olfactory sensations are a good indicator of what your angels are up to.

Meaningful Music

Angels can send messages through music.
https://pixabay.com/images/id-605422/

Have you ever heard music that inspired you so much that you started to feel like something better was coming? If you have been through a rough time and the lyrics touched your heart, or the melody just made everything seem right in the world, it could have been an angel singing to you. You may not think of angels having a voice at all, but they do have a way of expressing themselves through songs. It is also something we tend to give ourselves over to more easily than stimulation from the other senses, hence a very effective means of angelic communication. Some people claim they have heard celestial choirs while passing through state parks or even in their own backyard. Try listening to it next time as it is worth it if only to hear the sweetest sounds imaginable.

Messages in Dreams

Dreams are an effective way for angels to communicate. They can be very literal in nature or symbolic messages designed to tell us something that we need to know at that moment in time. Pay attention to what you experience in your dreams, and ask yourself if there is anything that needs to be addressed or made plain for you. The dream world is a very mystical realm, and our dreams can be a way for angels to talk to us. We should listen carefully because the messages are usually darkly poetic, but they are there if you know how to interpret them. These dreams also tend to be very intense, which is why we are so disoriented when we wake up. We are pulled back into our bodies, and the dream world starts to fade away. Sometimes the messages just come through in their entirety, but sometimes it is a matter of stringing together different things that are said to us over time.

Physical Symptoms

Your body constantly sends messages you may or may not pay attention to. Sicknesses, aches, and pains are signs that your body is giving off. These can be attributed to many things like stress, allergies, or our emotional state, but they could also be a way for angels to get our attention. The angelic realm sends vibrations through the atmosphere; sometimes, we pick up on those vibrations through physical pain. This is a sort of wake-up call that is designed to make us listen. The more we listen, the better we will understand. It is important to keep in mind that this should be taken into consideration with everything else. You do not want to assume every headache is an angel trying to make a point. You can best listen to your body and pay attention when it is giving off warning signals.

What Are Synchronicities?

Synchronicities are events or coincidences that seem to be meaningful. They appear to result from some cause beyond coincidence, such as intuitive causation. The word synchronicity was coined in the 1950s by psychologist Carl Jung. Jung noticed that people often experience coincidences related to their thoughts and feelings, and these events form a pattern leading to an insight or understanding. The events may seem random, but they often reflect a message that the person can use to understand something about himself or herself.

In many cases, this insight reveals some change in one's life direction or some opportunity. In such situations, the person feels they have gained an understanding of themselves or their life from this apparent chance meeting, encounter, or event. Synchronicity is the experience of meaningful coincidences resulting from divine guidance or spiritual meaning. Many types of synchronicities occur in almost everyone's life at some point. They can be triggered by a thought, feeling, or external events, and they can also occur randomly. Here are some common examples:

1. **A Meaningful Dream:** Dreams are internal events, allowing us to gain insight into our minds and feelings without outside interference. If a dream is particularly vivid and memorable, it may be trying to tell you something important. Dreams can also be prophetic or precognitive.

2. **A Coincidence That Seems to Be Triggered by One's Thoughts or Feelings:** Sometimes, you have a strong feeling that someone will call or visit, and they do. Things that are related to you in some way seem to turn up at the right time. You could be looking for something and find it right away, or have a need and immediately encounter the perfect solution when you least expect it.

3. **Fitting Circumstances:** Events that are related to the present situation are unusual enough to catch your attention and cause you to think, "That's strange." When something that seems out of place happens, we wonder why it occurred. If we remember dreaming about the event before it occurred, we may wonder if it has some meaning or message.

Synchronicity is an experience reflecting a spiritual order underlying the universe. Some people believe synchronicities result from divine guidance or spiritual meaning. It is thought that these coincidences are not random but rather purposeful interactions of the spiritual world. These events should be distinguished from mere coincidence, which does not have any sense of meaningful connection attached to it.

Synchronistic events are related, even if there is no apparent explanation for why they occurred together. It just feels as though there is some kind of connection between them. There is a certain amount of feeling involved in synchronicity, and we can often tell when something is meaningful to us, even if we cannot explain why it happened. When synchronicity affects you, you may feel excited and stimulated, as though something important has happened. You may also notice a sudden shift in how you perceive the world around you.

Synchronicity is a phenomenon that could be seen as one of the subtle, energetic ways that angels communicate with us. They are trying to wake us up to specific messages about ourselves or our lives by guiding us toward certain information and situations. Think of how synchronicities can kick start our lives in the right direction, showing us what we need to learn, whom we need to meet, or where we need to go. We may know something intuitively, think it over, and put it out of mind only for something relevant, significant, or important to happen. For example, you may have been thinking about returning to college but dismissed the idea because you had more pressing matters to cope with at work. However, soon afterward, you are offered a promotion or have a friend or colleague mention that they are considering going to the same college. Or perhaps you received an interesting brochure in the post, and it turns out that they offer an evening class which you could fit in with your work. This would be an example of synchronicity where something happens that is related to your thoughts and feelings but unusual enough to make you think, "That's strange."

Angels are trying to get us to pay attention and notice what may be guiding us. They want us to notice that there may be more going on than we realize, so we can make the most of the opportunities which come our way. They are trying to wake us up to the fact that our life is not as mundane and routine as we assume but may contain much more than we know. They want us to take note of things that don't seem to make sense and ponder what may be happening behind the scenes.

Angel Numbers

Angel numbers are a series of repeating numbers – often appearing at a significant time in our lives. They are a form of synchronicity and can be considered personal messages from your angels or spirit guides. But why would your angels want to deliver messages to you using a series of numbers?

Your angels and spirit guides are non-physical beings who exist at higher vibrational frequencies than we do. At this frequency, they do not experience the limitations of time and space as we do, so they can see everything in the present moment. They know us better than we know ourselves and see the bigger picture in our lives. They can see the purpose behind what we experience and know what we need to learn. They can also see the future, and for this reason, angels use numbers in their communications with us.

Angel numbers are everywhere, even on lottery tickets and license plates. These special sequences of numbers often appear at a time when we are making significant decisions or changes in our lives. Like all synchronicities, angel numbers seem to reflect some kind of spiritual meaning or significance behind them. The angel number series is used as a way for your angels to remind us of what we are here to learn or help us along the path we need to follow. For example, if you have a series of repeating numbers like 1111 and 2222, then this could mean that you need to pay more attention to the thoughts and feelings you have at these times.

How do you know when an angel number is trying to communicate with you? One of the easiest ways is by looking out for repeating number sequences. This could be 11:11 on the digital clock in your car or home or 11:11 on license plates as you drive past them. Sometimes they just appear in random places as numbers, or they could be a sequence of letters or words, but the most telling sign is if you realize that you have been thinking of and seeing a series of numbers recently. You may have been having lucid dreams or repeating words and phrases in your head that are represented by the number sequence. This repetition can be associated with an event or personal decision that has improved your life. If these repeated thoughts and feelings are related to an important turning point in your life, then you can be sure that these numbers were sent to you by your angels.

The extra energy the angel number series provides can help guide you toward making decisions and choices most aligned with your greater good. The energetic pattern of the number sequence is like an energetic fingerprint, providing you with a sense of reassurance and direction when making challenging decisions. For this reason, it is considered a sign from your angels, who delight in showing us how they are with us every step of the way.

Angel Numbers and Their Meaning

Numbers are symbolic and have been used as a form of divine guidance since the time of the ancients. They were often used in religious rituals and worship to address spiritual beings or entities, especially in medieval times. It is believed that these numbers were intended to aid the gods or angels as a means of communication by providing them with a physical form. Numbers also have a powerful impact on the human psyche. We can use them to communicate on many levels with the universe, and they can be used for things like making decisions, setting goals, or even healing.

When you notice angel numbers in your life, it indicates that your angels want to communicate something to you. They want to help put things into perspective for you and reassure you that all is well. They also act like spiritual bookmarks, directing your attention to a special page in the book of your life that needs reading. They are indications that a new chapter is beginning or that you have reached a significant turning point. Here is a list of common angel numbers and their meanings:

- **111** is the most commonly seen number sequence from angels, appearing everywhere from license plates to digital clocks. These numbers indicate that new beginnings are on the horizon, supported by the universal forces of attraction and expansion. It signifies that you are moving in the right direction and that your desires manifest before your eyes.

- 222 is also considered a significant spiritual number, as it represents your angels supporting you through all aspects of your life. This number sequence can indicate that you have made an important decision or choice that is in harmony with a greater purpose, one which will bring prosperity and new beginnings into your life.
- 333 is the angelic frequency associated with universal love and the soul's ascension. These numbers may appear anywhere, from hotel room doors to store receipts. They are common in synchronicities when an important decision is being made, and they tell you that love and compassion are powerful forces in the universe.
- 444 is another number often seen in synchronicity, representing the frequency of truth and purpose. It is also associated with physical manifestation, so these numbers can signify that your desires are manifesting into form around you. When you see these numbers repeatedly, they indicate that your angels want to help you to tune into the purpose behind what you are experiencing or where you are heading in life.
- 555 is the number associated with change and transformation. Often this is associated with an upcoming event such as moving to a new home or starting a new job. It is also thought to be the number of change and transformation in personal relationships, so it could be a sign that you must put more effort into communicating with others around you.
- 666 is often associated with the devil or evil, but this association is not accurate at all. This number has nothing to do with evil; it simply means "fear not." According to numerology, 6 relates to man, and when you combine it with fearlessness (12), you get a "fear not" message repeated twice. The fearlessness relates to the universal Divine perspective and the number twelve's connotations of perfection, wholeness, and completeness.
- 777 is a universal sign of achievement and fulfillment, associated with growth and expansion in every area of your

life. When you see these numbers, it means that you have overcome challenges in the past, and now you are moving forward into prosperity because of it. They may indicate that a great opportunity or reward is coming your way for all your hard work.

- 888 is the number of completeness. It signifies spiritual wholeness, divine connection, spiritual guidance, and freedom from constraints. When you see this number sequence, it indicates that you have attained conscious awareness and are receiving the guidance of your angels.
- 999 is a sign that your desires have been granted. It signals to all involved in your life that it is time to celebrate and often involves personal achievement or some form of recognition. These numbers indicate that you should take time to enjoy the moment because new opportunities will soon present themselves to you.

If you feel a little lost and confused, it may be the time to reach out to your angels. Whether or not you know it, they are there leading the way and trying to communicate with you. Look for the signs and if you cannot find any of them, ask yourself what is going on in your life right now that could use a little guidance. Then listen. Trust that they are there, even if they are not making themselves known.

Chapter Four: The Zodiac Angels

Zodiac symbols
Kwamikagami, CC BY-SA 4.0 <https://creativecommons.org/licenses/by-sa/4.0>, via Wikimedia Commons: https://commons.wikimedia.org/wiki/File:Zodiac_circle_(planetary_colors).svg

While most of us are not zodiac sign-savvy, we have all heard of the concept. Zodiac is a term for the constellations of stars visible in the night sky. There are 12 zodiac signs, each of which has an archangel and several guardian angels who watch over those under them. The concept originates from astrology, which purports that cosmic correspondences exist between celestial bodies in our universe and people on Earth. These twelve constellations move backward through the night sky, completing one full circle in a year, and are visible in the Northern Hemisphere. The concept of the Zodiac is a very ancient one, dating back to ancient Babylon, but it has been used in different forms in almost every civilization. To understand your zodiac angel's true meanings and how it can affect your life, you need to be familiar with its primary qualities as an energy source. The stories behind each celestial being and its influence domain will tell you much about your character and potential. We will begin with a quick overview of the zodiac signs:

Aries: Aries is the first sign of the Zodiac, representing a life focused on action and adventure. The characteristic of Aries is a single-minded focus on what needs to be done, even in the face of opposition or danger. You are inclined to take risks, but an edge to your aggressiveness can land you in trouble. However, you are persistent and do not give up easily when achieving your goals. When you do succeed, though, it is probably because of your tenacity. Those born under this sign love to prove themselves, and they will succeed in many ways, but their dominating, domineering attitude gets in the way of their relationships, which may come off as selfish and demanding.

Taurus: You were full of potential and enthusiasm in your early years, maybe a little too much of both at times. You may have been unconventional and a bit subversive. You had incredible ideas but could not always follow through with them because you tended to get stuck in the planning stages. You have matured over time and learned to let things play out by themselves rather than planning them every step of the way. Your life energy has undergone a similar transformation, finally finding its own path rather than trying to control everything all at once.

Gemini: Your life has always been very complex, and you have always had to think on your feet, adapt to new situations, and improvise. You thrive on challenge and love change, new experiences, and being in the middle of things, at least when they are positive. When it comes to negative stuff, you tend to avoid it. You have a gift for conversation that others find refreshing. You never lie or evade the point. You always say what is on your mind, but this can come out in blunt statements, which can be hurtful.

Sometimes you talk so much that people get annoyed with you, but nobody can ever doubt your dedication and talent for communication.

Cancer: You have always been sensitive, perhaps too much so. You may have painful triggers in your life, especially if you suffered from abuse when you were a child. Even now, you take on people's pain as if it is your own. You need to learn to let go and learn how to protect yourself from situations that can be perceived as a threat but really are not. You need to learn to trust yourself and what you know about the world around you. In some cases, this may involve reevaluating your beliefs. Over time, you have learned to take care of yourself rather than relying on the moods and demands of others. You are intuitive and have a way of knowing what is right for you and what is not. You always follow a feeling in your gut.

Leo: Your life has always been about the big picture, but in many ways, it has been about pride more than anything else. You have high standards and a sense of moral obligation regarding justice and integrity. However, you must be careful that this does not come across as bossy or rigid because others can take it that way. You have to let things flow the way they are meant to rather than forcing them into a preconceived idea of how they should be. You must learn to trust others and let them grow at their own pace.

Virgo: This signifies service, hard work, health, and healing. You are so focused on the details and practicalities that you may miss out on bigger issues. It is important to look at the big picture in your life and be flexible when it comes to dealing with others. You like things neat, tidy, and well-organized, and, as a result, you may feel overextended sometimes. You may not have time to talk about things that matter to you, but you always have time to do specific and necessary things. You are an expert on details and practical things, which gives you a strong value system. However, it can be difficult for you to revel in your accomplishments, so sometimes it helps to take a step back from the day-to-day and just breathe.

Libra: Your life energy is balanced and harmonious but also flexible and creative. You are sensitive to your feelings and intuitive about people's intentions. The ideal Libra partner is someone who can be totally supportive and will not try to rush into commitment or force through change. You need a partner who is willing to work on the relationship, who will give you a lot of space and let you live your own life. You also tend to be practical and down-to-earth regarding others' opinions or values since your goal is always peace, harmony, and balance. This can lead you to compromise too much.

Scorpio: This sign is associated with passion, depth of emotion, and hidden desires. You can be combative at times and have great power potential. Sometimes this power is channeled into anger or frustration. Other times, it can move people into action for the greater good. You have been hurt before and know how it feels to be on the receiving end of pain. You are usually very aware of others' feelings, and you tend to put yourself in their shoes, putting your own needs on the back burner. You also have a sharp mind, with a laser-like focus on detail and nuances that other people are not so good at picking up on.

Sagittarius: Your life has always been one of adventure and excitement. You love the outdoors and are a bit impulsive. You like going off the beaten path, even when it means taking risks, not necessarily dangerous ones, but more choices or options that help you keep things exciting in your life. You like to expand your mind, keep up with the latest trends and ideas, and try new things. You are a risk-taker, but in a good way. You have never been afraid to do what seems right or just.

Capricorn: This is a sign associated with ambition and pride, the need to achieve, sometimes at the expense of others. You want the best for yourself and for those you love. You thrive when you have a challenge with plenty of material resources. You like stability and control but also enjoy getting together with large groups of people, but only if it is important to you. However, this may come across as selfishness or self-centeredness and can cause conflict in some situations. You like structure and order in your life, and you can be very persistent. You also tend to be on the conservative side when it comes to relationships. You believe it should always be planned and romantic, making you appear cold or snobbish.

Aquarius: Your life has always been about change, adventure, mystery, and connections with the world around you. You are a free spirit who loves traveling, exploring, and meeting new people from different backgrounds. However, this could also make you vulnerable to getting caught up in bad situations or people who are not good for you. You have a harder time committing to people and letting them entirely into your life, especially if you feel as if they are not living up to your expectations. At times, you can be inappropriate with people's emotions and may have trouble taking things seriously. You need to learn that for a relationship to be successful, it needs to be built on real love and commitment.

Pisces: This is a very sensitive and creative sign, which can lead you to be moody, hesitant, unpredictable, and not always sure of what you want. You like to feel connected to spiritual and cosmic forces and are often drawn toward the arts. You think deeply about life, death, love, and the details of your own personal relationships. Your creativity can lead you to have difficulty following through on plans that you have made, and this can frustrate you. When it comes right down to it, it's all about feeling emotions and connecting with others through those emotions. You can be intense and reserved, so you must learn to connect with others through communication and honesty. Speak your mind, be true to yourself, and let others do the same.

Corresponding Zodiac Angels

Malahidael of the Aries Zodiac

Malahidael means "One of courage" and is the sign's ruler, Aries. He symbolizes all energy and power and is a great inspiration for action and adventure. He is the angel of life and transmutation and is known to be strong yet gentle and kind toward others. Malahidael is portrayed as a warrior angel, and his color is gold or orange. He is closely accompanied by Ariel, the Angel of Instinct, a lesser-known guardian of the Aries Zodiac.

Asmodel of the Taurus Zodiac

Asmodel is the angel of Taurus and aids in teaching self-worth, courage, and balance. He is known to be a wise and powerful mentor who inspires us to reach higher levels of consciousness. His colors are red or orange, symbolizing strength, perseverance, longevity, and vitality. Asmodel supports the preservation of Nature through the wisdom that comes from spiritual teachings. He stays connected with the Earth Mother and is closely accompanied by Chamuel, the Angel of Compassion. Together, they provide the strength and courage needed to fulfill the quests of the Taurus, who may sometimes have difficulty finding their way in this world.

Ambriel of the Gemini Zodiac

Ambriel is the angel of Gemini and aids in teaching communication, action, and relationships. He also teaches spiritual lessons to assist us in developing our own inner wisdom. His color is silver or gray, and his energy can be described as cold yet emotional, mysterious, and charming. Mental clarity, awareness, and a dose of laughter and joy are vital to his teachings. He is accompanied by Kadiel, the Angel of Expression, who works closely with him to provide guidance and protection to those seeking it. Their energy combines to promote enthusiasm, creative thoughts, inspiration, and understanding to the Gemini.

Muriel of the Cancer Zodiac

Muriel is the angel of Cancer and aids in teaching courage, intuition, and awareness. She is known to be courageous, protective, and passionate in her teachings. Her color is green or blue and symbolizes a high level of wisdom. She teaches life lessons that give us the tools necessary to overcome our fears and create a feeling of safety and serenity. Muriel is also known as the angel of unconditional love and an energy healer. She uses her energy to balance the Cancer's emotional and intuitive feelings and manifest positive outcomes in all areas of their life.

Verchiel of the Leo Zodiac

Verchiel teaches us the importance of service, unity, and communication. He is also known to be brilliant, quick-witted, and intelligent, if a little eccentric at times. His energy can be described as playful yet powerful. His color is silver or red and symbolizes the element of fire. Verchiel teaches the power of faith, intuition, and self-worth to those who invoke him through prayer. He is closely accompanied by Raziel, the Angel of Mysteries and Secrets, who aids in revealing spiritual growth to those who ask for his assistance. Together, they work to bring about the highest level of awareness, manifestation, and power for all Leos.

Hamaliel of the Virgo Zodiac

Hamaliel teaches patience, health, and understanding. He is also known as the holy angel of flowers, herbs, and peace. His color is green or silver, and he can be described as introspective and wise.

He teaches us to live in the present rather than dwelling on the past or worrying about the future. He is closely accompanied by Anael, the angel of truth and knowledge, who aids in illuminating the inner-self with understanding. The combination of their energies helps the Virgo Zodiac to reach the highest spiritual level of development, self-worth, and understanding.

Zuriel of the Libra Zodiac

Zuriel teaches us to live in service to others. He is also known as the holy angel of balance, truth, and knowledge. He is seen as a teacher of understanding, equality, and justice. Light blue or white (the colors of his wings) represents wisdom and truth. He teaches lessons that help us to heal through giving, as well as helping us to regain our natural state of happiness by communicating with others. Zuriel also teaches the concept of intuition by imparting lessons that open up our minds and hearts to seeing beyond what we know. He symbolizes both emotion and intellect, qualities accurately embodied by the Libra.

Barchiel of the Scorpio Zodiac

Barchiel is the angel of Scorpio and teaches lessons against lust, possession, and jealousy. He takes an intense interest in war, power, and all things of the mind. However, he also teaches that we must develop an acceptance of our own capacity for pain or suffering. His color, black or dark red, symbolizes power and knowledge. He lives in dark or intense energy and can be very persuasive in his teachings. For the Scorpio, he brings the light to illuminate the darkest corners of their mind. He teaches awareness of what is real and what is not. He is closely accompanied by Asmodel, who is the angel of Taurus, which represents the element of earth and helps to balance Barchiel's energy of power.

Adnachiel of the Sagittarius Zodiac

Adnachiel teaches us about the importance of love, happiness, and optimism. He is also known as the angel of power and independence. His energy is described as joyful, playful, and always seeking fun. He teaches us to connect with others deeper, helping them find their inner power and divine nature. He can also teach us about the patience, faith, and determination that are needed to rebuild our lives after a painful experience. His energy is golden or orange and represents solar energy and the element of fire.

Adnachiel is closely accompanied by Zadkiel, who teaches about action, initiation, and freedom. Together, they can teach the Sagittarius about letting go of the past and healing from emotional trauma.

Hanael of the Capricorn Zodiac

Hanael teaches us the importance of love, hope, and wisdom. He is also known as a holy angel of acceptance and surrender. His energy is seen as intense, serious, and wise. He teaches us to surrender our fears and desires, change what we can accept and what we cannot, and have faith in life's lessons. Hanael guides us to apply our own unique gifts to help others in times of need, rather than allowing our personal needs to get in the way. His colors are royal blue or purple. Those who invoke him are said to be blessed with divine help that leads them to inner peace, prosperity, and happiness. He teaches the Capricorn to forgive themselves rather than judge.

Kambriel of the Aquarius Zodiac

Kambriel teaches us to live in a state of freedom and reject all things symbolic of limitations. He is known as the angel who can help us find our true purpose in life. He also teaches about patience, adaptability, healing, and the reality beyond what we can see with our earthly eyes. His energy is seen as pale blue. Together with his partner, Uriel, he can show the Aquarius that their past is not a burden to carry but rather an important part of their journey to enlightenment. He also teaches them to live in the moment rather than dwelling in worry about the future.

Amnitziel of the Pisces Zodiac

Amnitziel teaches us about responsibilities and commitment to others. He is also known as the angel of romance, passion, and psychic abilities. His energy symbolizes positivity, inspiration, and balance. Those who invoke him experience happiness and live in the present moment. Amnitziel imbues wisdom, strength, compassion, and integrity into his teachings. His color is blue or purple, representing the universe, angels, and higher consciousness. He is closely accompanied by Zaziel, the angel of guidance and knowledge. Together, they teach the Pisces that their dreams can come true and that love is more than just a feeling.

Chapter Five: Communicating with Your Guardian Angel

What are guardian angels? Are they spirit beings or physical entities? Do they have a set job description or responsibility? What can you do to attract one into your life? These are all questions everyone has wondered at some point in their lives. The guardian angel concept was first brought to public attention in the 1800s by a French poet named Ernest Psichari. Since then, interest in guardian angels has grown and sparked debate worldwide on what they are, what they do, and how people can connect with them.

To understand guardian angels, you must first look at the contrast between religions or belief systems that believe in them and those that do not. Some religions do not believe in guardian angels at all, while others use this concept as one of their central tenets. In either case, the different perspectives on guardian angels are intriguing.

The guardian angel is viewed as a spiritual entity that upholds the divine order of things by caring for those entrusted to it. The guardian angel takes care of people while they are alive and, depending on the belief system, after death. Some guardian angels are also viewed as a special set of helpers who have been chosen and assigned to care for people whenever they are needed. In this case, the chosen angel is treated as a personal guardian who, when called upon, does not simply do what is asked of them but also takes care of the person regardless.

Guardian angels are believed to have been created by God before the creation of humans, and it is believed that there is at least one guardian angel for each person. It is also believed that each guardian angel has different roles. For instance, some of them are assigned as healers, others are protectors, and some serve as messengers between humans and God.

Although guardian angels have been used by many religions to explain away unexplainable phenomena or to answer a prayer request, only Christians significantly believe in guardian angels. For Christians, the archangel Gabriel is known to be a protector and guide, while Michael is known as a defender against evil forces and an advocate against temptation. The guardian angel is said to be the Holy Spirit or God's emissary working right beside the person who was assigned them. The angel is said to not only help during times of need but also to send messages from God, fulfill prayers, and show itself to people in times of trouble. However, for Christians, guardian angels are also assigned at the time of birth and can change as the person's role in life changes.

The guardian angel concept is referenced in various religious texts. For instance, it is found in the Bible and in ancient Greek, Hindu, Persian, and Assyrian texts. These texts speak of angels who work to guide human beings in their lives and who, when they need assistance, do so in a very passive fashion. In other words, the guardian spirit is only there to help out if someone needs their help. They are never intrusive and do not step in unless it is necessary.

According to Hindu texts, guardian angels are associated with the gods and viewed as manifestations of godly powers. They are believed to be personified forces of nature and elements that keep all things in order, and they perform their duties in harmony with the laws of nature. They are said to be given orders by the gods, but they are believed to have free will and decide how to carry out their commands.

As mentioned earlier, not all religions believe in the concept of guardian angels. This applies to non-theistic religions, such as Wicca, Pantheism, and those who believe in reincarnations. Instead, they are believers in spirit guides, a concept that is closely related to guardian angels. As with guardian angels, spirit guides are designed to be there for humanity and also do their best to help people succeed on their journey to greater spiritual understanding or enlightenment.

Guardian Angels in Esotericism

In esoteric circles, a guardian angel is any nonphysical entity protecting a person from harm or negative thoughts or emotions. What makes this form of a guardian angel unique is its ability to bring positive thoughts and ideas into your life by changing your perception of things around you. For example, a guardian angel can be used to change your thoughts about an argument with someone or your fears of a certain situation. They also come in handy when something bad happens to you, such as when you are in danger or need healing. In these situations, it is believed that the guardian angel intercedes and draws out the best version of you so that you do not have to fear what is happening to you. In such cases, the nonphysical being is responsible for the circumstances in which these things happen so that they are beneficial to the human involved.

There are different levels of guardian angels according to esoteric belief systems. For instance, in some understandings, the more evolved guardian angels that have already been sent to Earth only watch over you, and you can call on them for help at any time. In other belief systems, this is the first level of a guardian angel's existence, and when these spirits are considered to be older and wiser, they may listen to your thoughts and feelings and use it as a guide when helping you through life. As they grow in their expertise with you, they can make more proactive choices based on what you need at that time. You can also use these spirits to get advice on decisions that you need to make and how you can find the best alternative options for those decisions. Some esoteric groups also believe that everyone is assigned a guardian angel from birth. Here, it is considered the guardian angel's responsibility to guide their "protégé" throughout his or her life to achieve their full potential. It is believed that these entities are assigned to each person due to their life goals and reason for incarnation in this world. The guidance can come in various forms, from dreams to thoughts or even different intuitive feelings that may seem unusual at first but can all help you understand things about yourself and the world around you.

Getting in Touch with Your Guardian Angel

To begin a relationship with a guardian angel, it is suggested that one should begin with the more basic techniques of meditation. This can be done daily in the morning or evening. Once you meditate, getting in touch with your guardian angel or spirit guide may be easier. There are different ways to approach this relationship. It can start as a simple friendship or partnership that involves talking to the nonphysical entity and then moving into a more active phase in which the entity willingly helps you out on some level.

With guardian angels, it is believed that they have already chosen you and are already looking over you. However, they may need your help understanding what they can do to help you. If this is true, all that needs to be done is to open your mind and be receptive to such assistance. Meditating will also allow you to achieve an altered state of consciousness that will allow your guardian angel to communicate with you in a way that works for both of you. This is often simply a conversation between the two of you where one or both parties want certain things from one another. The key, however, is to believe that you will be heard and understood.

Suppose you require healing or assistance with a certain situation. In that case, you can ask your guardian angel for help, although it may take longer to get a response from them. This type of communication is more one-sided in that it involves someone asking for assistance or help with something, and then the being will respond as needed. It can be as simple as just a feeling that something has changed in your life since you prayed for help.

It is also believed that our guardian angels are always around us and constantly use their energy to protect us from harm. Here, it is considered to be important for us to trust our angels and let them know that we are aware of their presence and appreciate their help. If you are having a bad day or have recently been in an accident, you can ask a guardian angel for help at that moment. A way to open up communication is by saying the words "I need your help" or "I want your help." This will then allow the entity to work on helping you, which may be through sending some message through intuition or just through helping you to feel better.

The Power of Meditation

Meditation makes it easier to connect with your guardian angels.
https://unsplash.com/photos/rOn57CBgyMo?utm_source=unsplash&utm_medium=referral&utm_content=creditShareLink

Meditation is a technique that involves clearing your mind of thoughts and allowing intuition to come to the fore. If you are not familiar with this technique, it is simply the act of sitting quietly and focusing on nothing but your breath until you notice something new coming into your awareness. At this point, do not attempt to control or direct what thoughts come into your consciousness. Instead, simply watch them float by like clouds in the sky. It is believed that you can use this technique to develop a communication channel with anyone, including your guardian angel. This is simply a method of relaxation and meditation that will allow you to feel one with the universe in a very literal sense. Here, no words or thoughts need to be exchanged between two parties when using this method of communication. Instead, "feelings" will flow to and from your consciousness, allowing you to understand what the other being is trying to convey.

It is believed that when you are in a state of meditation, you are more receptive to messages from your guardian angel. Therefore, your guardian angel can communicate with you through meditation and other intuitive techniques. It is also believed that during meditation, it is possible for things of a spiritual nature to be sensed, although these spirits are not always voices or thoughts that can be easily understood. However, a common experience that one may have while meditating is when the body, mind, or soul feels lighter or different for the duration of the practice. You can also include guided meditation in your practice. This is where you go through a series of instructions from a recording or from another person. It allows you to relax your mind and focus on breathing, which will disconnect your conscious thoughts from the inner self.

How to Meditate

If you are interested in meditating, it can be as simple as taking the following easy steps:

1. Find a quiet place where there is likely to be no interruption.
2. Change into comfortable clothing and shoes.
3. Light a candle to put you in the mood for meditation. You can also use music or surround yourself with soft colors and gentle scents like lavender, sage, or rose petals.
4. Sit with your palms facing upward in your lap.
5. Close your eyes and breathe deeply into your diaphragm area. Diaphragmatic breathing will allow you to focus on the moment rather than on any other thoughts floating. Your breathing should be slow and controlled. Inhale through the nose while counting to two, hold this breath for two more seconds, and then exhale slowly out the mouth.
6. Continue breathing this way until you are comfortable with the process.
7. Do not struggle with any thoughts or images that may be floating around. If they come into your consciousness, simply let them pass by and continue with your breathing.

8. Once you are comfortable, invite your guardian angel to the room.
9. Ask for any messages or guidance from your angel.
10. See what images or thoughts come into your consciousness. This may take time, and there is no rush to make things happen.
11. When you have finished, imagine the light that comes from your guardian angel spreading over you until it fades away and leaves you feeling centered and relaxed.

You must keep the link between your conscious and subconscious minds open. This is known as the "flow of thought," and it allows your conscious mind to send messages and thoughts through to your subconscious mind. If too much information is coming from one channel and not enough from the other, it may result in confusion or even anxiety. However, when things flow smoothly between both channels, it will allow you to get in touch with your intuition and inner core self in a very literal way.

Other Ways to Contact Your Guardian Angel

Meditation is a great way to communicate with your guardian angel, but it is not the only technique out there. There are other ways that you can send messages to your guardian angel, and here are a few:

1. **Prayer:** Praying to your guardian angel can be extremely beneficial, and it is considered helpful to make a specific request rather than simply asking for help or guidance without giving any information. Here, you can put your request into words or write a prayer that includes what you want and thanksgiving for any help that has already been received.
2. **Writing:** When you need your guardian angel's help, you can write down your thoughts and concerns. Once you have completed writing, put the piece of paper away in a safe spot. This way, it does not require any action on your part to maintain your thoughts without forgetting them. You can also write down what it is that you need help with or ask for guidance or insight surrounding the issue at hand. In the

following days, look out for any messages or signs that seem unusual or outside the norm. These can be from your guardian angel or other helpful entities.

3. **Visualization:** Visualization is the act of picturing something that you want to happen or something you need. Here, you can visualize what you want to happen and project this intention out into the universe. Once you have a clear picture of what it is that you need, it is believed that this picture will trigger your guardian angel to come to your aid. The picture will then appear in dreams and other forms of communication from your guardian angel.

4. **Pilgrimage:** A pilgrimage is more difficult to undertake than the other techniques, but it is believed that by walking along a path that has special significance for you, you can communicate with your guardian angel. This can also be done by going on walks in places that are significant to you or your spiritual experience. As with the other methods, you do not try to direct or control your thoughts. You simply let them go where they may find the answers that you seek.

5. **Telepathy:** Your spoken communication with a guardian angel may take the form of "telepathic" communication. This is where it differs from other alternative forms of communication that are common and accepted within mainstream belief systems. Here, actual words are exchanged between the two parties, but nobody can hear those words or understand what is being said. It can be as simple as one party just sending off messages and images to the other without anybody else knowing about it or being involved in the communication process.

Maintaining the Angelic Connection

Once you have interacted with your guardian angel, you should be open to a continued relationship with them. In this way, even if you are not actively thinking about them or their existence, being in contact with your guardian angel can still benefit your life. Here is how you might maintain a connection:

- **Relish the Good Feelings:** You can positively reinforce the positive feelings that come from connecting with your guardian angel. When you find yourself experiencing these good feelings, gratitude for these emotions should flow readily into your life.
- **Be Aware of the Signs:** If you have contacted your guardian angel and have been receiving help, it is important to know the signs they may send your way. While it may take a while to get used to trusting that your guardian angel is helping you, it is important to begin looking for signs of their existence. If you can begin recognizing these signs, you can also begin rewarding yourself with kind thoughts and gentle words.
- **Record the Experiences:** If you are having a lot of interaction with your guardian angel, it can be helpful to make notes about what you are experiencing. This will help you better understand how helpful your guardian angel is, how often you communicate with them, and the types of things they help you with. It will also allow you to better recognize signs from them and understand their existence in your life.

The Importance of Gratitude

It is very important to show gratitude to the guardian angel that has been helping you along your journey. Even though you have endured negative or unfortunate circumstances, it is very important to remember that you were guided into these situations. Turn your disappointments into lessons and celebrate the moments when things work out for the best. Showing gratitude for all that happens to you allows your guardian angel to feel appreciated and continue to help you when you need it. One way to show gratitude is by acknowledging your guardian angel's presence and thanking them for their role in your life.

You can also show your gratitude by blessing others who are going through difficult circumstances. If someone is having a hard time, you can offer them words of encouragement and show them that you support them. You can even bless others by praying for them or sending them positive energy. You can also show gratitude by giving thanks for the gifts that you have in your life. This could be the gift of family and friends, health and shelter, food, water, and everything else you have and feel grateful for.

Chapter Six: Connecting with Angelic Beings

In chapter five, we talked about guardian angels, what they are, and what they do for us. In this chapter, we will explore ways to contact any angelic being. Please note that not all beings have the same capabilities, and messages can be conveyed in several ways. These beings are generally found in the angelic realm, an expansive place, so preparing before you venture out there is not a bad idea. When working with an angel, it is important to understand that they can appear however it is most comfortable for them.

It may help to have a question or request in mind when you go out looking for angels. It is also important to remember that not all beings can interact with humans, and among those that can, not all of them will. You must also be open to the possibility of seeing things or undergoing experiences that may not make sense or seem logical. Angels can be quite playful, so it is a good idea to keep an open mind and know that you are on a journey of discovery.

To begin your search, pick a spot where you feel comfortable and familiar. Remember that all information is energy, so to get the best results, work in a space that is clean and clear of clutter. The area should also have good lighting and be well ventilated. I recommend that when you are speaking with an angel, you should be sitting comfortably and relaxed. Having a journal and pen next to you for notes is helpful. You'll also want to ensure that you are physically comfortable, so wear something loose-fitting and soft like cotton.

It is best to start with a prayer or meditation to help center your energy. Being centered will help you remain open and focused. Once you enter this space, it is important to remember that there are no mistakes here; it does not matter if you do not "feel" anything the first time out. Remember, this is a process of discovery not just for yourself but for the angelic beings.

The Importance of Spiritual Protection

Before you begin your search, it is important to consider your spiritual protection. We all come into this world with a predetermined level of protection, depending on our karma. The three basic layers of protection are:

- Our physical bodies
- The energy field (or aura) around our bodies
- The chakras or energy centers in our bodies

The physical body normally provides the first layer of protection from birth until death. However, we can influence this by poor lifestyle choices such as eating poorly, not hydrating enough, not getting enough rest, and so on. This is why we need to take the best care of ourselves physically, to remain in the best health possible. The second layer of protection comes from our auras, which help to keep out any negative energy. If the aura is cleared in or around the body, then it is easier for us to cleanse and heal since there is nothing to block our energy. One of the best ways to clear auras is through Reiki, which can be done quickly and easily. Another thing to remember about auras is that they change daily, and it takes time for them to recover.

The third layer of protection comes from the chakras, which are like psychic batteries that help keep our energy flowing freely. When we have blocked energy, the chakras are like useless batteries. To use them again, they need to be charged. This is best done through meditation and other forms of energy work. When clearing auras, it is best to clear each chakra in turn, starting with the base (root) chakra at the bottom of the spine. This will help to reset blocked energy and give you a boost of energy. During clearing sessions, it is also important to remember to let go and be gentle, as even the best intentions can cause harm if done improperly.

Before venturing into the spiritual realm in search of angels or for any reason at all, your protection should be priority number one. This is especially true when you are seeking to connect with angelic beings. The reason for this is simple, angels can see a person's entire aura, and they can read your life story like a book. The more they can see, the more they will know about you. This can be either good or bad depending on whom you are speaking with and whether they like what they see. You'll also be vulnerable to any negativity that wants to penetrate your auric field.

Many techniques can be used to provide a shield of protection, and these techniques have been around for thousands of years. Different techniques work for different people, so keep trying until you find one that works. Among the most popular protective techniques are:

1. **Performing a Ritual Bath:** This is a great way to purify both the aura and the physical body. It is also a way to bring in good, loving energy. I recommend you perform one of these baths at least once a month or more often if you feel the need. Use the time to meditate while you are in the water and say a prayer before entering and exiting the bath. You'll need a large bowl or container of water, some sacred oil, and a candle to start this. Begin by lighting the candle, and then take your time to run your bath and light a little incense. When the water is ready, slowly enter the bath without splashing. Begin to relax and allow the water to flow over you. Keep your eyes closed as you lower yourself into the water. Let as much energy flow through as possible, and do not be afraid to completely let go if it feels right for you. When you are ready to get out, slowly ease yourself out of the water and climb onto the towel or mat. After you have finished your bath, avoiding contact with other people is advisable until after communicating with the angels because their energy can interfere with your cleanse.

2. **Creating an Energy Field:** This protective shield can be created by performing a meditation where you draw in positive and negative energy and create your own personal

shield around yourself. If you are feeling disoriented or off-balance, this is also a great way to tone down your aura so that it is not so strong and overpowering. For angelic encounters, it is best to have this shield of protection around you at all times instead of just creating it when you need it.

3. **Using Crystals:** Crystals are wonderful tools to use for protection. They can help to maintain a flow of energy and block unwanted energies from entering your energy field. In addition to this, they can also keep different spiritual energies from interfering with each other. Some of the most common crystals used for protection include onyx, black obsidian, clear quartz, pyrite, black tourmaline, and amethyst.

4. **Visualization:** Visualization is a great way to enhance your spiritual protection. Visualizing an energy field around yourself can help maintain a buffer of protection that will keep negative energies from entering your aura field.

5. **Cleansing Your Space:** Cleaning your home and removing clutter from your life is a way to create more space for positive energy in your life. The less clutter you have in your home, the more energy you'll have for yourself. It may be time to clean out some of those stuffed closets and remove things you no longer need or want. This is a great way to increase your aura's clarity. You can also smoke your space with herbs like sage, incense, or palo santo.

This is not a complete list of all the ways to increase your spiritual protection. It's important to keep trying different techniques until you find one that works for you. As we get older and our worldview changes, we may also have to adjust what we use for protection. Finding what works for you is a process of trial and error, but this could also help you to discover new techniques that will work better.

Ultimately, it is not just about what techniques we use but how we use them. Having the right intention behind our actions is just as important as how we act. The more we can be at peace with ourselves internally, the better chance we can connect with angels. An angel's job is to help us maintain a state of mental, emotional, and spiritual balance, so the more we keep our intentions pure and in harmony with the universe, the easier it will be for them to come through. In addition to this, we should also work on building more positive energy into our lives by doing things that are good for us. This will help increase the positive energy around us and consequently attract angels that want to help us maintain this balance. Now that we have covered protection and set the stage, let us get down to business by considering some ways to make contact with angels.

Establishing a Line of Communication

The idea of communication with an angelic being is quite mystical, especially if you are not a believer in spiritual beings. This is perfectly understandable because no matter how much we understand the universe, there is still much more to learn and explore. However, some very simple steps can be taken to increase your chances of having a positive experience while searching for angels.

First and foremost, it is important to keep an open mind because if you do not, you are only setting yourself up for failure. After all, most of us have been taught to dismiss things we do not understand, which can lead to some very closed-minded thinking. Having an open mind involves being ready to consider all the possibilities, not just the ones we are comfortable with. With an open mind, you are more likely to see the truth and not be afraid of it. When you have an open mind, angelic communication is much more likely because it is only *after we are certain* that something is possible that we can invoke angels. Letting go of anxiety and being willing to explore new things is a great way to increase your chances of connecting with beings from other worlds.

Another thing that you can do to increase your chances of making contact with angels is to spend time in nature. I would recommend spending time outdoors in nature and going on frequent walks. This will help you relax and clear your mind so that you can listen to what the universe is telling you. Nature is a place where we can feel the presence of God, and this connection is something to cherish. Some people find it easier to connect with angels when they take long, hot baths or spend time meditating alone in their home, but you may want to give nature a try as well.

Finally, get rid of all distractions because this will help create an atmosphere conducive to reaching out and making contact with a spiritual being. If you want to make angelic contact, you must be completely focused on the task. It can be nearly impossible to achieve this if you are surrounded by a lot of noise and chaos in your life. The less clutter in your mind, the better chance you have at opening yourself up fully to what the universe is trying to tell you.

One of the most important things that you can do to increase your chances of connecting with angels is to be happy. This is not just an idle statement either, as it is easy to assume that we will quickly be able to attract happy spirits into our life if we are only blessed with happiness itself. The reality is that it takes a great deal of effort to maintain happiness in your life. It is not something that comes easily but involves working at making yourself happier. You can work at doing this in many ways, and the most important is by setting intentions. You can set an intention to be happy, healthy, at peace, or whatever you want to create in your life.

You may believe that you must put in a lot of hard work to find your angels. However, it is important to realize that achieving happiness only takes a bit of intention and hard work each day. You do not have to spend the rest of your life working on yourself because once you have made it, wellness will become a permanent part of your life. It is not something that you have to struggle with, and it is also not something that is going to go away. In the same way that a master chef can prepare a delicious meal in minutes, taking only minutes each day to focus on making yourself happy is enough to improve your health and wellness.

I mentioned earlier that there are many ways that you can make contact with angels, but we will focus on two specific cases, meditating on the angelic realm and getting an angel reading. Both of these are methods for reaching out to angels and making them more available for you.

How Can You Communicate?

Meditation: There are many forms of meditation, with the most popular being Transcendental Meditation. TM is a technique that involves you sitting relaxed with your eyes closed and focusing on breathing from your belly. Your focus is on one object, and your thought processing should be kept to a minimum at all times. When you meditate, it is vitally important not to try to control the content of your thoughts because if you do, you'll be focusing on yourself and not the entity you are connecting with.

One of the things that you can do to find more information about meditation is by reading what other people have had to say about it. This is a great way to get tips on meditation techniques that work best for you, and it is also a way of increasing your own understanding of the techniques. Meditation has proven time and time again to provide benefits of all kinds, including better stress management, overall improvement in life, and even better health.

Pendulum Reading: This is a form of angelic reading. There are many different types of pendulums with varying styles and purposes. Pendulums can be used in many ways ranging from simple pendulum magic to very complex rituals involving spells and rituals. The purpose of using a pendulum is to relay information that you would typically not be able to get by first-hand observation only. You ask the question, and then the pendulum goes into action, indicating the answer. This is a great way to discover who your guides are and how they want you to move forward.

Pendulums can be used to find out if someone is preventing you from moving forward in life or whether it is only a matter of direction. Pendulums can even be used to try and guess the kind of work you are meant to be doing in life. If a pendulum gives you a number, it is up to you to decide how this number relates back to reality.

If you are unfamiliar with pendulums, try finding one that feels right. A pendulum can be any item that is on a string or cord, such as a ring, crystal, or wood. Choose an object that has special meaning to you and holds some of your own energy. Hold it in your hands and allow yourself to become attuned to its energy. When you are ready, sit quietly, close your eyes, and reach out with all of your senses, seeking any vibrations from the Angelic Realm. Focus on every sensation and feeling you experience as if it is something of great importance. After 5 to 10 minutes, take the pendulum out, and you'll be ready to start getting answers to the questions you have in your mind.

If you are a beginner at this, it is best to keep things simple and connect with one or two energies rather than connecting with every angel that may be around. If you try and do this all at once without guidance, it will not work well for you at all. The interpretation of the pendulum's movements must be agreed upon before any communication begins. For instance, you can tell the pendulum to swing forward for YES and backward for NO, or vice versa, i.e., backward for yes, and forward for no. Now, wait for the pendulum to respond in agreement with your request, and if the pendulum swings back and forth between each request, you are on the right track. If not, give it a few minutes and try again.

Once you have agreed on how to interpret the movements of your pendulum, begin asking questions. You can ask basic yes or no questions at first, such as, "Is anyone here with me?", "Am I doing this right?" or "Is this the right time to ask these questions?" If you do not receive any response, then stop using your pendulum and try again later. With practice, you will be able to proceed to more complicated questions.

Tarot Cards: The tarot is an ancient divination and fortune-telling tool used by many people across the world. It can effectively reach out to your angels and receive answers to questions you may have. Some people find it easier to connect with their angels through tarot cards because the images are so clear and accessible in a way that many other forms of meditation are not. The connection you make with the card becomes a focal point that helps you begin receiving information from the angels.

Tarot cards can help you effectively reach out to your angels.
https://unsplash.com/photos/eUX74J_IpXw?utm_source=unsplash&utm_medium=referral&utm_content=creditShareLink

When using tarot cards, practice being present. Pay attention to everything you are experiencing as you try to interpret the images you see on the card through your senses. If a card shows a person, ask who is depicted in the image, how old they appear to be, and their role in your life. If there are symbols such as stars or masks, then begin to focus on their meanings. If the image shows a tree, then ask yourself what kind of tree it is and what it symbolizes for you. When you are ready, ask your angelic companions to give you answers to the questions that you have regarding the cards that you have seen.

Crystals and Gemstones: Crystal reading is a form of angelic communication that utilizes crystals and gemstones. Crystal readings are an excellent way to connect with your angels because they are versatile, illuminating, and beautiful. They help your angels to be able to speak directly to your mind, and you find that their answers come in quick-moving bursts of information in a flash. If you have not used stones or crystals before, you must begin by connecting with the crystal you selected before trying to go further.

Once you have found a crystal that works for you, then it is time to work on the technique. You need to close your eyes and imagine a figure representing the angel you are trying to communicate with in your mind's eye. Then, simply sit quietly and ask the spirit of your crystal to communicate with the angel you have asked it to try and reach. If you can, have your stone on hand or nearby to be within easy reach. The answers will come in any form which may be relevant to the person asking the questions. For some people, this may be through words or sentences, but for others, it might come in through a feeling or sensation. Sometimes the answers may not be in words or feelings but in an image or memory. The answers may also come as signs or symbols that have special meaning for the person asking them.

The best way to learn about crystals and gemstones is to find out what kind of experiences you have when you are with them. If, after a few weeks of trying, you discover more about yourself through the stones, then this is a good sign that you are on the right track with your communication.

Invoking an Angel

Invocation is another form of angelic communication which involves the summoning of an angel to help you through your problems. Invocation can be a powerful means of bringing about change in your life. However, it has some rules, rituals, and guidelines you should follow if you want to ensure that your message is received by the angels and not some other spirit or entity.

Step One: Begin by creating a ritual space where you can do this invocation safely and effectively. You can do this by turning off all the lights and lighting some candles, creating a sense of mystery and spirituality. Place any relevant crystals and gemstones on your altar, as well as any other items such as pictures or statues that help inspire your meditation. Select an area in your home where you feel most comfortable, such as a quiet room where you'll not be disturbed.

Step Two: Now, prepare yourself for the invocation. This can be done by washing your hands and face, wearing clean clothing, and fresh fragrant flowers that you have picked yourself. You then need to focus on the angels you want to communicate with. Take a moment to consider what it is that you need help with and why. Make a mental list of all of your concerns to form a coherent message for the angel in your mind's eye.

Step Three: Moving forward, you need to face your altar and begin to meditate. If you have been doing this practice before, you'll know what it feels like to have a vision of an angel standing right in front of you, although if you have never done it before, this is your chance to learn. Picture the angel in whatever way works best for you. Some people find it easier to visualize a small child, and some people use angels from the scriptures, although whichever way you do it, you need to be able to imagine clearly and vividly. It is important that you maintain contact with the angel by focusing on them, even if for just a few moments.

Step Four: When you feel that you have made the connection clearly, then ask for an answer to your concerns. When there is a reply, determine how well you can understand it. Often the answers come in symbols or images which require interpretation on your part. Take your time and try to figure out what the image or symbol means for you. Then cast a circle by drawing a sacred symbol on the floor in front of you, protecting against any harmful forces that may be trying to break in.

Chapter Seven: The Archangels of the Four Corners

The Jewish tradition teaches us that, to keep the world in order, God assigned four special angels the responsibility of watching the earth's four corners. Having such a task was not easy, and the angels were given special powers that would help them protect their designated corner. Michael, assigned to the South, was bestowed with the power of fire. Gabriel, the keeper of the West, was given control over the element of water. Raphael, who guards the East, was given charge of the wind. Finally, Uriel, who watches over the North, has command over the Earth. The Jewish prayer, Kriat Shema, written and read three times a day by all orthodox Jews, asks for protection from these four angels. The prayer contains the names of each angel associated with the element and corner of the Earth he guards. It is basically a call asking for Uriel's protection from the north, Raphael's from the east, Michael's from the south, and Gabriel's from the west.

The shamanic practice of calling on these four archangels was brought to Europe by Jewish refugees from Spain and Portugal who fled the mass exodus in 1492. The study and teaching of these four archangels are now widespread throughout all segments of Judaism (Orthodox Judaism) and to a lesser degree within all Indo-Aryan religions.

The belief that angels are at each of the four compass points can be found in numerous cultures worldwide, including Native American tradition. There are certain elements common to all of these traditions. The four cardinal directions, north, south, east, and west, were all considered special in the ancient world, and each is associated with its own unique deity. Each direction is considered the guardian of an element, which governs a specific sphere of human activity. In neo-paganism, this tradition is currently experiencing a renaissance, reflecting a growing interest in the esoteric traditions of our ancestors. In addition to the protection offered by these special angels in the east and west, time was divided into four seasons, each ruled by its own guardian, also known as an archangel. In Hebrew lore, Michael is the guardian of spring and summer, Gabriel is associated with autumn, Uriel is the guardian of winter, and Raphael presides over spring.

The four Cardinal Virtues (Temperance, Fortitude, Justice, and Prudence) are named after the four archangels. Our ancestors highly valued these virtues as a key to living an ethical life. God was known to embody these virtues, just as the four angels were known to watch over the cardinal points. Temperance was closely associated with Michael, Fortitude with Raphael, Justice with Gabriel, and Prudence with Uriel. While these virtues may not be well-known in popular culture, they are still part of our collective consciousness and are being taught in synagogues and schools worldwide.

Angels, like human beings, are themselves composed of various elemental parts. The four elements are:

- Earth (Geburah)
- Wind (Tehinnah)
- Water (Hod)
- Fire (Yesod)

These correspond to the physical body, emotions, ego, and intellect. Working together, these four make up our entire being. When each is not balanced with its corresponding element, it becomes imbalanced, causing disharmony and imbalance within our lives. When a person is unbalanced, it reflects in their lives. Unbalanced emotions lead to destructive, even murderous behavior.

An unbalanced ego results in an inflated sense of self, which leads to violence and arrogance. An unbalanced intellect can result in betrayal and cruelty toward one's fellow man. The angelic guardians of the elements act as a balancer, restoring harmony and balance when one's element is unbalanced. With the imbalance of one of these elements can come illness, depression, fear, and hopelessness. The guardians of the elements are not there to cure these illnesses but rather to help restore order and balance.

In the Jewish tradition, the angels are also associated with the four worlds of existence, Atzilut, Briah, Yetzirah, and Assiah. When one achieves harmony within these four worlds, one will ascend to higher levels of spirituality, moving closer to God. This practice falls under the umbrella of Jewish mysticism and is considered to be an intermediate level between beginner and advanced practice.

The first documented association between Michael, Gabriel, Uriel, and Raphael with their respective elements was in an essay called "The Book of Life," written by Isha Schwaller De Lubicz. It took place in 1907 at the annual congress of occultists worldwide. In this essay, he described how each angel was associated with one or more of these elements. The idea was further developed in the 1940s by Samael Aun Weor, who wrote that the four elements and the four cardinal directions were spiritual forces resembling a circle's quadrants. They were responsible for creating an invisible whirling vortex within the universe.

Moving counterclockwise, they created a continuous cycle of manifestation, creation, preservation, destruction, and dissolution. They were also believed to contain a fifth element, which was the "Tetragrammaton" or "Sha-He-Vau-He," the sacred name of God. This is the source of all life, and it is recounted in Genesis as one of only four letters needed to construct the universe. The five-pointed star is a symbol of these five elements. In the Jewish tradition, this symbol is called "The Shield of David" and is one of the most prominent symbols of Judaism, along with the menorah. It is a reminder that there is only one God (Sha-He-Vau-He).

Archangel Michael, Guardian of the South

In the western tradition, the symbols associated with Michael are the eagle and the color red. The eagle is a symbol of transformation and selflessness. In Freemasonry, it is considered to be a symbol of immortality and rebirth. In alchemy, it represents fire and thus transformation.

Fire was considered by our ancestors to be an essential element in life and was believed to hold all potential within its transformative power. Michael is the guardian of the element of fire, known as Geburah. The color red symbolizes fire's creative and destructive power, associated with its fiery nature. It is a symbol of war, violence, and rage. However, when it is balanced, it can be associated with selflessness, courage, and strength.

In the Bible, Michael is said to have appeared in front of the prophet Daniel to help him understand a vision he had seen. He also appeared before King Solomon to help him choose between two women who claimed to be the same child's mother. In Islam, he is known as "Jibril" and is one of the seven angels standing before God's throne. He is a warrior angel who has been sent to defend the faithful as a commander of God's army against evil. The Qur'an informs us that he revealed to Mohammed the location of Paradise and Hell. He is represented by a sword and a pair of wings, symbolizing his role as one who carries death but also medicine and life.

In the qabalah, Michael represents Gevurah, one of the ten sephirot on the Tree of Life. Gevurah carries a variety of meanings in Hebrew, ranging from restraint, strength, and power. Also associated with the element of fire, it is considered to be a force that is necessary for the balancing of all other forces. Thus, Michael is referred to as being "the prince of peace" since he brings an understanding of the law by helping one reconcile with oneself and one's own internal conflicts. He represents the ability to come to terms with hard facts in life and not act out on impulse.

- **Color:** Michael is most associated with the color red, which is known as the color of fire. The color red also symbolizes strength, vigor, and passion. In Freemasonry, blue is associated with Michael. Blue is seen as an emblem of light, purity, and constancy. In Christianity, it is symbolic of heaven and immortality. Green is also associated with Michael because he represents nature.

- **Chakras:** The chakras of Michael are said to be in the pituitary, adrenal and solar plexus. The pituitary is associated with ego-consciousness, the adrenal with emotions and passions, and the solar plexus with instinctual energy. Each of these three areas has a chakra at each point. The hormones associated with these areas impact our behavior and reactions to situations. Michael is said to help provide balance when they are imbalanced.

- **Planets:** Michael is associated with Saturn because he is the guardian of the element of Geburah. According to ancient astrology, Saturn's influence was thought to bring about a greater understanding of reality and a gradual change in consciousness. The color associated with Saturn is red-gold.

- **Sun Signs:** Michael is associated with the sun sign Leo. As one of the three fixed signs of the zodiac, Leo is known as the sign of self-expression and ego. It is also a fire sign.

- **Vibration:** Truth, authenticity, and selflessness.

- **Crystals:** Blue sapphire, golden labradorite, sodalite, and lapis lazuli are crystals that can be used to help ground Michael's energy.

- **Symbols:** The symbol of Michael is a golden eagle with wings spread – a symbol of protection and regeneration.

- **Invocation Tip:** The best time to invoke Michael is during the summer months at 11:11 a.m. and 11:11 p.m. When invoking Michael to help put you in a state of receptivity for his energy and messages, it is helpful to contemplate the symbology associated with Michael, such as the eagle.

Archangel Gabriel, Guardian of the West

Gabriel is known as the messenger angel, who symbolizes communication and the regulation of our interaction with others. In the Christian tradition, he is most well-known for bringing the messages of God to both humans and angels. His name means "God is my strength," which is a positive quality associated with him. He represents God's power, which is evident in his name, "Gabriel," which means "God's hero." In Islam, he brought news of God's revelation to Mohammed and instructed Daniel on how long the exile would be. He is associated with the color green, which symbolizes the growth of life. He has the power to reveal divine light and is considered to be a healer and teacher who helps us grow spiritually.

In Qabalah, Gabriel represents Keter. Keter means "the crown" and is one of ten sephirot on the Tree of Life. As the crown, it sustains creation as it evolves through its many cycles of manifestation. It is also associated with God's ability to create without limit or bounds and with His ability to permeate all creation and everything in it by His divine breath (Vau). Thus, it is associated with inhalation, inspiration, and resurrection. Considered the angel of mercy and love, Gabriel helps us develop these qualities in our lives and grow. "*The angel who unites the Creator with all created things, who mediates between heaven and earth*" is how Rabbi Shlomo Yitzchaki described him.

- **Color:** Gabriel is associated with the color green, which symbolizes growth and renewal.
- **Chakras:** The chakras of Gabriel are in the crown and throat. The throat represents our ability to communicate, and Gabriel's role as the messenger of God means that he can help us learn how to speak clearly and effectively, as well as make our voice an instrument for good.
- **Planets:** Gabriel is associated with Uranus. Uranus is a planet that represents the discovery of our true nature. It can be seen as a struggle between two opposing forces, the desire for freedom and individuality and the need for security and community. It is associated with many colors, including green, purple, blue, yellow, black, and musical notes.
- **Sun Signs:** Gabriel is associated with Aquarius because of his association with Uranus. Aquarius is thought to represent strong individuality, the liberation of self-

expression, and a new dawning of consciousness. It also represents an individual's ability to remain independent of outside influence, which can be contrary to desire or necessity.

- **Vibration:** Truth, love, and abundance.
- **Crystals:** Green sodalite and lapis lazuli are crystals that can be used to help ground Gabriel's energy.
- **Symbols:** The symbol of Gabriel is a two-winged angel with a trumpet. The two wings represent his role as a messenger of God, and the trumpet represents the message he brings.
- **Invocation Tip:** To invoke Gabriel's energy, meditating on the symbols and colors associated with him is useful. It is also useful to find a green object or a picture of a green-winged angel and place it where you'll see it frequently. When in prayer, you can invoke his energy by calling upon him to help you communicate effectively, making your voice an instrument of good and delivering messages from God.

Archangel Raphael, Guardian of the East

Raphael is the messenger angel of healing who brings us divine knowledge. He is associated with the color purple, which symbolizes the power of healing and wholeness. His name means "God has healed," and this healing quality has favored him greatly during his long association with humanity. He is associated with compassion, mercy, and unconditional love (Rah). In the bible, God tasked him with ministering to the Israelites after their exodus from Egypt, and he assisted Tobias in his journey back to his homeland. He also assisted Abraham in crossing the Red Sea. He exemplifies patience, persistence, and self-control as a role model for humanity. His healing role is reflected in his association with Venus, the planet of love and attraction.

In Qabalah, Raphael represents Chokmah. Chokmah is the second sephira on the Tree of Life and is associated with wisdom. It represents the active side of knowledge and experience. It is considered to contain everything that exists in potential, including all opposites in their perfect balance, as well as being able to give birth without limit or bounds. Thus, it is associated with inspiration, the breath of life, and resurrection. Raphael helps us grow spiritually through his healing qualities and compassion for humanity. He can help us become more introspective and sensitive to the problems of others so that we can better understand their issues from a compassionate point of view.

- **Colors:** Purple is the color of healing, and Raphael's role as the angel of healing means that he can help us become sensitive to and receptive to his healing influence.
- **Chakras:** The chakra of Raphael is in the heart, representing our compassion and ability to love others.
- **Planets:** Raphael is associated with Venus. Venus is a planet that represents love, refinement, and attraction, and these qualities represent his healing energy.
- **Sun Signs:** Raphael is associated with Taurus because he is associated with Venus. Taurus is known for its steadfastness and perseverance in working toward its goals, which reflects Raphael's desire for humanity to continue working toward spiritual perfection.
- **Vibration:** Forgiveness, health, and joy.
- **Crystals:** Amethyst and jadeite can be used to cleanse and open up Raphael's subtle energy centers.
- **Symbols:** The symbol of Raphael is a purple circular disk surrounded by angelic wings.
- **Invocation Tip:** When preparing for a healing session is the best time to invoke Archangel Raphael.

Archangel Uriel, Guardian of the North

Uriel means "God is my light," and his name symbolizes the integration of spirit and matter. He has aided humanity in its spiritual evolution since the early days of creation, when he is said to have helped Noah build the ark after the great flood. In Egypt, he was the leader of a group of angels who protected and helped humans while Pharaoh enslaved them. He also helped Moses to escape Egypt with the Israelite people.

In Qabalah, Uriel represents Netzach. Netzach is one of ten sephirot on the Tree of Life and is associated with our ability to suffer or endure earthly existence to fulfill our goals. It is also associated with attraction, restoration, and renewal. Uriel, who aids spiritual evolution, can help us in our personal spiritual growth through his ability to help us endure suffering and life's challenges. He can also help us to regain our strength and resolve, through which we can achieve our goals.

- **Colors:** Yellow is the color of Netzach and is associated with Uriel's tranquility and wisdom.
- **Chakras:** The chakras of Uriel are in the throat and third eye. The throat represents communication, which is an important part of spiritual awakening. The third eye represents our ability to see beyond the physical world into a higher plane of consciousness.
- **Planets:** Uriel is associated with Jupiter. Jupiter is a planet that indicates expansion, relationship, and stability, and these qualities represent his healing energy. It is also associated with many colors such as yellow, blue, red, green, white, and violet (light blue).
- **Sun Signs:** Uriel is associated with Gemini. Gemini is known for its quick and adaptable mind, which attributes to the importance of communication during spiritual growth. He is also associated with Aquarius because of his association with Uranus. Aquarius is known for their detached sense of individuality, freedom, and change, which reflects his role as a guide in our spiritual evolution.
- **Vibration:** Truth, faith, and higher purpose.
- **Crystals:** Smoky quartz or yellow calcite can help activate Uriel's energy in the subtle bodies.
- **Symbols:** The symbol for Uriel is a blue circular disk surrounded by rays of gold.
- **Invocation Tip:** You may feel Uriel's presence in the middle of meditation or quiet contemplation when you are on the verge of opening up to another level of consciousness.

Chapter Eight: More Archangels and How to Work with Them

Archangel Azrael

In western tradition, the symbols associated with Azrael are a cup and a scythe. The cup symbolizes introspection and reflection, while the scythe represents transformation. The cup represents Christ's words in Christianity: *"I came not to bring peace but a sword."* This statement was meant to show that we must fight our own inner demons to be able to make spiritual progress along our path.

The scythe is an instrument that is used in harvesting crops and reaping death, especially through war or pestilence. It is a symbol of death but also of transition and renewal. According to alchemy, the scythe represents aging and renewal. Azrael is often called the angel of death since his duty is to bear the souls of the dead and guide them into their new life.

He is also described as being associated with Saturn, which in ancient astrology was thought to represent an inner strength or maturity that produced a change in one's consciousness. The power attributed to both Saturn and Azrael has been considered necessary to make progress on one's path toward enlightenment. In

Buddhism, Amitabha Buddha is portrayed holding either a cup or a jewel in his hand. This is about Azrael, who is considered Amitabha's attendant.

In the Kabbalah, Azrael is associated with the sephirah Binah. Binah is known as the mother of the universe and is representative of understanding and wisdom. It represents a personal relationship with God and a sense of trust in God's care for oneself. Azrael also represents the eleventh hour of Malkuth, which means to be an expression of divine power in the physical world. As such, he can also represent time, especially that which has elapsed since one's birth or rebirth into this life.

- **Color:** Azrael is associated with the color black. Black symbolizes power, authority, and judgment. According to Hinduism and Buddhism, it represents death.
- **Chakras:** The chakras of Azrael are in the heart, throat, third eye, crown chakra, and base chakra.
- **Planets**: Azrael is associated with the planet Saturn. This planet's association with time has made it an appropriate choice for this angelic representative since Azrael serves as the custodian of time during one's entire life span on Earth. As such, he represents the law of karma and destiny as well as divine justice and divine mercy that attends us throughout our lifetime. The color associated with this planet is silver-white.
- **Sun Signs**: Azrael is associated with the sun sign Scorpio. Scorpio is known as the sign of regeneration, death, rebirth, and transformation. Because this sign is a water sign, it has a deep connection to the unconscious mind and to psychic processes. This connection has led others to associate it with magic and sorcery. Azrael is also associated with the sun sign Sagittarius. Sagittarius is known as the archer and represents directness, honesty, and freedom of expression. It also represents an ability to see a situation from many perspectives, which can help one understand truth and make wise decisions based upon that understanding. The color associated with this sun sign is gold.

- **Vibration:** Light, wisdom, and inner change.
- **Crystals:** Black obsidian, jasper, chrysoberyl, and red garnet are crystals that can be used to help ground Azrael's energy.
- **Symbols:** The symbol of Azrael is a scythe and cup. As stated above, this represents the reaping of death through war or pestilence while also representing the reaping of death through natural forces such as aging, disease, and death itself. Azrael's symbol is also a feather. Feathers have been used to help connect the earthly realm with that of angels by providing a medium for transmitting messages. In Hinduism, the word for feather is said to be *aksa*, representing the power of flight. It also represents the power of inner awareness as well as spiritual aspirations. Feathers also represent wisdom and spiritual power in many Native American tribes. In Aztec culture, Azrael is referred to as The Feathered Serpent and depicted with talons and feathers adorning his body. The Feathered Serpent represents life, death, rebirth, and evolution through a transformation because it sheds its skin every few years.
- **Invocation Tip:** The best time to invoke Azrael is during the fall. He can also be invoked during new moon rituals. It is helpful to contemplate the symbology of Azrael when invoking him to help put you in a state of receptivity for his energy and messages.

Archangel Chamuel

Chamuel is known as the angel of love and compassion. His name means "He that sees God" and refers to his ability to simultaneously see the past, present, and future. Chamuel acts as an envoy of God's love so humanity may achieve spiritual progress by dealing with its darker passions. He is one of the angels who preside over Taurus's zodiac sign, characterized by its reliability and perseverance or tenacity. It is represented by the element Earth, which symbolizes stability and dependability. Taurus also represents those things that are tangible and physical and is associated with body and matter.

Chamuel has a healing effect on human consciousness, especially with understanding how negative emotions can be transformed into positive energy. As a representative of introspection, he helps us transform our internal emotional life and our relationship with others while helping us understand how we can heal emotional wounds that have occurred in past lives and in this lifetime. He can help heal and transform the heart, enabling it to be more open to love and wholeness. As the angel of love, he works with Archangel Sandalphon to form the angelic order of archangels known as the Elohim. He is exalted above all creatures in his knowledge of God and his power to heal human suffering.

Chamuel's positive energy can have a powerful healing effect on ailments related to the respiratory system (i.e., asthma, bronchitis) and those related to hormone production (i.e., infertility and impotence). Those who work with Chamuel often find their ability to manifest wealth at all levels greatly enhanced. Chamuel's energy can also help one work through the more difficult parts of past lives to attain a greater sense of peace and spiritual wholeness. As the angel of peace, he teaches one how to achieve inner peace and balance during difficult circumstances.

- **Colors:** White, purple, and gold.
- **Chakras:** The chakras of Chamuel are in the heart, head, solar plexus, and third eye.
- **Planets:** Chamuel is associated with the planet Mercury. This planet is associated with communication, intellect, mental function, education, and learning. It also represents a higher spiritual life, which is highly connected to the power of intuition. The color associated with this planet is silver-white.
- **Sun Signs:** Chamuel is associated with the sun sign Taurus.
- **Vibration:** Compassion, understanding, and transformation.
- **Crystals:** The Herkimer diamond is a crystal that works well with Chamuel.
- **Symbols:** Chamuel's symbol is a caduceus or staff with two serpents wrapped around it. He is often depicted holding a

branch in his left hand, which represents the healing of physical ailments through the power of compassion. The other two snakes are symbolic of healing the wounds of the past.

- **Invocation Tip:** The best time to invoke Chamuel is during the winter solstice and during new moon rituals. He can also be invoked during planetary transits such as Mercury, Venus, and Mars.

Archangel Raguel

Raguel's name means "friend of God." He is known as the guardian angel of the planet Earth and represents divine justice. He is believed to be the guide of souls who pass through the underworld on their way to heaven. Like a guardian angel, he works with both humans and animals. Sometimes, he is depicted with animal heads, for example, a dog or a lion. In these forms, his function can also be seen as that of a protector and messenger between heaven and earth. Raguel helps us discover our divine will according to what we need in our spiritual path so that we might find increased happiness while fulfilling our own unique mission. Raguel's energy is also closely allied to that of Chamuel in that he helps us learn how to use our emotions positively and how to overcome their negative expressions in our lives. He teaches us how to deal with anger, hatred, lust, and other worldly desires to find greater peace within ourselves. In addition, he teaches us how to radically accept love from the divine realm into our own lives because of the spiritual power it holds for self-awareness.

In the Bible, Raguel is mentioned in the book of Isaiah. He appears as a prophet who witnesses the destruction of Babylon and participates in Jesus' coming into the world. The symbol of Raguel depicts the beaded cord he carries around his neck, which is the mark of his prophetic mission and divine authority. As a prophet, he often has a relationship with God on behalf of humanity. He may also be given assignments to protect and defend particular people or places.

In the qabalah, Raguel is the archangel of the sephirah of Netzach. The sephirah Netzach is associated with emotions, instincts, and the force that unites thought with action. His symbol is two overlapping triangles, one pointing up and the other pointing down. This symbol represents the union of heaven and earth as well as the union of matter with spirit. Netzach also represents those things that come into being through conflict. It is connected to feelings, desires as well as sexuality, and secret passions.

- **Colors:** Blue, gray, and silver.
- **Chakras:** The chakras of Raguel are the heart, throat, solar plexus, and third eye.
- **Planets:** Raguel is associated with the planet Uranus which is linked to abstract ideas, freedom, and autonomy. It can also be associated with creativity, metaphysics, science fiction, extraterrestrials, and technology. Raguel is also linked to the planet Mercury, known for communication and intellect. The color of this planet is silver-white.
- **Sun Signs:** Raguel is associated with the sun sign Gemini.
- **Vibration:** Peace, understanding, and transformation.
- **Crystals:** Citrine, aquamarine, and carnelian
- **Symbols:** Raguel's symbol is a staff or wand with letters on it that spell out his name in Hebrew letters and his title, "friend of God," as well as an eye in the middle. The staff, which serves as a symbol of the divine, is related to justice and protection. The letters which spell his name in Hebrew on the staff's shaft remind us that we must be willing to speak up for what is right. The eye at the center of the staff represents knowledge, purity, and God's watchful presence.
- **Invocation Tip:** The best time to invoke Raguel is during the winter solstice and the waxing moon. Invoking him on Mondays, Wednesdays, and Fridays is also good. He can also be invoked during planetary transits such as Uranus, Mercury, and Venus.

Archangel Zadkiel

Zadkiel is the archangel of freedom, mercy, forgiveness, and gratitude. Often depicted with a sword in his hand or a sword sheathed at his side, he is said to be the highest angel of grace. In addition, he is seen holding grapes or ears of wheat in his hand to represent divine nourishment for the soul. Zadkiel's role can also be seen as that of a teacher who guides us on our spiritual path and encourages us to embrace God's gift of universal love, divine forgiveness, and spirituality within our daily lives. He can be invoked to help us to understand how the past governs our present lives and how we are always connected to the divine realm.

In the qabalah, Zadkiel is the archangel of the sephirah Binah. Binah is associated with understanding and enlightenment. It is related to thought, intelligence, and memory. Zadkiel's symbol is a crown with two cobwebs, representing divine illumination. In addition, the sephirah of Binah also represents divine action and purpose.

- **Colors:** Violet
- **Chakras:** The chakras of Zadkiel are the heart, throat, and third eye.
- **Planets:** Zadkiel is associated with the planet Jupiter, known for growth, expansion, abundance, and good fortune. Jupiter's color is yellow-gold.
- **Sun Signs:** Zadkiel is associated with the sun sign of Libra, representing balance and harmony as well as relationships and love. He is also associated with Sagittarius.
- **Vibration:** Spiritual connection, mercy, and charity.
- **Crystals:** Clear quartz crystal.
- **Symbols:** Zadkiel is often depicted with a sword. The symbol of the sword represents divine protection. It also represents the divine power that frees us from our own ignorance and arrogance to embrace divine wisdom, love, and sympathy for others.
- **Invocation Tip:** The best time to invoke Zadkiel is during the winter solstice when the light comes into the world. It is good to invoke him on Mondays, Wednesdays, and Fridays. It may also be good to invoke him during planetary transits such as Jupiter, Uranus, and Mercury.

Archangel Jophiel

Jophiel is the archangel of wisdom, purity, and love. He is associated with the feminine aspects of the divine realm because he is often depicted as an angelic maiden. His presence can be felt in the ascent of the soul to the heights of self-awareness, spiritual power, and transcendence. He can be invoked to help us to understand how we can move beyond the search for knowledge toward a greater understanding of ourselves and how we are pure equals in divinity. In the Kabbalah, Jophiel is the archangel of Chokmah. Chokmah is associated with divine intelligence, intuition, and awareness. Its symbol is a flowing river that represents creative inspiration. This sephirah also represents our connection to the world of ideas.

- **Colors:** Yellow and green
- **Chakras:** The chakras of Jophiel are the heart, solar plexus, and third eye.
- **Planets:** Jophiel is associated with the planet Venus, which is associated with creativity, love, and happiness. It plays an important role in relationships and can also be linked to the element of water. Its color is yellow-green.
- **Sun Signs:** Jophiel is associated with the sun sign of Cancer, known for sensitivity, love, and compassion. He is also associated with the sun sign Scorpio, which is known for power, leadership, and sexuality.
- **Vibration:** Pure love, knowledge, and self-awareness.
- **Crystals:** Kyanite and amethyst crystals can be used to work with Jophiel.
- **Symbols:** Jophiel's symbol consists of three dots or circles which spell out his name in Hebrew letters and his title, "friend of God," in English. At the front of this symbol are two wings representing spiritual illumination and empathic understanding of others.
- **Invocation Tip:** The best time to invoke Jophiel is during the spring equinox when the light of the divine realm comes into the world. It is also good to invoke him on

Mondays, Wednesdays, and Fridays, but he can be invoked at any time.

Chapter Nine: Prayers and Meditation

Prayer is a form of communication with God or any spiritual entity. Prayers can be as short as one word, but they can also be very long and detailed. It allows us to ask for help, give thanks, connect with someone or something in spiritual or emotional ways, and get closer to God. Prayer is universal. It is practiced by many faiths and cultures in many languages and styles.

Meditation is a time to calm your mind, focus on one thing, and become more aware of your environment and self. It can be practiced as a daily routine or used as a tool for healing, relaxation, or personal insight. Meditation allows us to focus our minds on one thing at a time, rather than being bombarded with external stimuli like other sounds or people. Focusing inward and being aware of our bodies, thoughts, and feelings may help us gain insight into who we are as human beings and enable us to reach angels for assistance.

Much of what we need in our lives comes from the universe, but how do we ask for it without sounding silly or naïve? The answer is prayer and meditation. Not only does it help us to better express ourselves, but it also helps us to connect with God and the angels on a deeper level. It is a way to acknowledge the source of all our needs and let them know that we want whatever they have to offer that could be useful to us.

Prayer to Archangel Michael

This prayer is best said on Sunday, the day dedicated to the Archangel Michael. The prayer will begin with an acknowledgment of the angel and gratitude for all he does. Then, pray to ask the archangel for his divine protection, strength, guidance, and wisdom in all aspects of your life. Ask him to be with you as you begin the new week and grant you the strength and courage to face the week's challenges. Ask for protection from all evil entities and request blessings upon yourself, your family, and all people. The prayer should end with gratitude as if your requests have already been granted. Use a few moments of silence to ground yourself before concluding the prayer.

Prayer to Archangel Gabriel

Monday is dedicated to the Archangel Gabriel, and this prayer would be best said on that day. This prayer asks for the archangel's divine protection and energy to help you bring joy, beauty, and happiness into your life. Ask him to guide you through the work week so that you may find peace and happiness within yourself. Request that he help you clear negative thoughts, energies, or people out of your life so that joy may continue to flow into your life. End the prayer with gratitude and praise, as if your request has already been granted. A few seconds of silence is ideal for grounding yourself before going about your day.

Prayer to Archangel Uriel

Tuesday is dedicated to Archangel Uriel, so this prayer should be said on that day. This prayer is for those who may feel unsure about their direction in life or their future. Ask for Uriel's divine protection and assistance, as well as his guidance and wisdom, so you may gain clarity about your future path. If you are struggling with a particular aspect of your life, ask for his help to release it from your life so that you can move forward in the most positive way possible. Acknowledge his presence in your life, then end the prayer with gratitude and praise, feeling as if your request has already been granted.

Prayer to Archangel Raphael

Wednesday is dedicated to Archangel Raphael, so this prayer should be said on that day. This prayer is for those who are struggling with negative thoughts or people in their lives. Ask for Raphael's divine protection and wisdom as well as his guidance and assistance throughout your week so that you can be more receptive to joy, beauty, and happiness in your life. Ask for help releasing negative thoughts, energies, or people from your life so you may find peace and happiness within yourself. Acknowledge his presence in your life as well as his energy and blessings. End the prayer with gratitude, then allow a few moments of silence to ground yourself before concluding the prayer.

Prayer to Archangel Selaphiel

This prayer should be said on Thursday. The prayer is to ask Selaphiel to help you achieve a healthy balance of love and work. Ask for a balance of your heart, mind, and spirit and help balance your love life. You may also desire help balancing work and play to be more productive. Pray for his divine guidance in your personal relationships or with coworkers. You may also wish to pray for his guidance as you search for a life partner or if you are feeling lost and alone. The prayer will end with gratitude and praise, feeling as if your request is already granted before going about your day. Acknowledge his energy and guidance, as it will help to balance the forces of light and dark within your life.

Prayer to Archangel Raguel

Friday is dedicated to archangel Raguel, and the prayer should be said on that day. This prayer is for those who may feel restless, unfulfilled, or alone even though others surround them. Ask for Raguel's divine protection and assistance as well as his guidance and wisdom so that you may find inspiration and clarity about your life path. You may also need help finding your purpose or balance in your personal relationships and careers. The prayer will end with gratitude, acknowledging that your request has already been granted before going about your day. Acknowledge his presence in your life, as it will help to inspire you and keep you focused on achieving goals.

Prayer to Archangel Barachiel

This prayer should be said on Saturday. The prayer is to ask Barachiel for his divine protection, energy, and guidance during the weekend. Ask for protection from all evil entities and assistance to remove that which is not of the light from your life so that you may be inspired and guided to continue moving forward in your journey. You may also wish to pray for help regaining faith in yourself or others and help to resolve personal issues from your past, so you can move forward with a clean slate. The prayer will end with gratitude and praise, feeling as if your request has already been granted before going about your weekend.

The above examples of prayers to angels provide you with a basic template of what prayer to angels may look like. However, you must personalize this in a way relevant to your needs or desires. You can change the angel's name according to which day you are saying the prayer, or you can add or remove certain aspects of the prayer. Use what you believe will work best for you and fit into your lifestyle. The angels can be called upon at any time to help us achieve our goals and achieve peace within ourselves. We may receive divine inspiration and guidance when it is most needed through prayer. Allow the angels to work with you in whichever way suits your needs. Pray and be open to receiving the answers that you seek.

Other Helpful Prayers

Prayer to Overcome Addiction

You may pray for help in overcoming addiction to any substance or substance. Pray for the strength and endurance to overcome the addiction and the willpower to resist that substance. You may also wish to ask for help in dealing with feelings of shame, embarrassment, guilt, and self-loathing. Perceive yourself as strong and courageous in this struggle. Feel your power as you heal from a deep place inside of you. The angels and God are with you in this process. You can also ask Archangel Michael to help free you and your loved ones from addiction. The following steps can be followed for a meditative exercise to assist the process:

Step One: Relax your mind and body. Take a few deep breaths, tune into your body, and relax.

Step Two: Imagine the energy of addiction leaving your body. Feel it leaving your body, through the top of your head, and out through the bottom of your feet.

Step Three: Imagine a strong light surrounding you and falling like rain, completely covering you in the light. This image will help to neutralize any negative effects that the addiction may have on you.

Step Four: Thank God for this opportunity to heal and release yourself from this bondage.

Step Five: Let all past feelings of shame, embarrassment, or guilt fall away with the energy of this healing. You are forgiven. You are free. You have the power to change your life and heal yourself.

Step Six: Thank the angels and God for your freedom. You can add any other meditations or prayers to this exercise if you want, such as asking to have visions of your desired outcome of healing from addiction or asking for protection from the addiction in question.

Prayer to Overcome Negative Thought Patterns

You may pray for help to overcome negative thought patterns that seem to keep repeatedly playing in your mind, preventing you from experiencing peace of mind. Pray for the strength and endurance to overcome these thoughts, wisdom, and guidance so that they no longer control your life. Ask Archangel Raphael to help you replace the negative thoughts with positive thoughts. Pray for help in breaking the cycle of negativity in your life. You can use meditation to assist in the process of transforming this negative energy into positive energy. This can be done with the following steps:

Step One: Relax your mind and body. Take a few deep breaths, tune into your body, and relax.

Step Two: Focus on breathing in a way that allows you to relax more each time you inhale and relax more each time you exhale.

Step Three: Turn your attention to your thoughts and note and describe negative thoughts that keep coming into your mind.

Step Four: Using the above prayer to Archangel Raphael, ask him to help cleanse you of all negative energy so that these thoughts no longer control you. Ask him to help you see them for what they are, the past and not the future. Feel his divine light surrounding you, allowing you to see clearly with Divine guidance.

Step Five: Give gratitude for this opportunity for healing and release yourself from this bondage.

Prayer for Peace of Mind

You can pray for help in achieving peace of mind. Pray for the strength and endurance to overcome anxiety and stress. Ask Archangel Raziel to help you use your mind to create a peaceful, tranquil environment around you. Pray for help to eliminate the causes of anxiety. Ask Archangel Uriel to help you overcome your fears. Let the angels and God guide you as you make changes in your life that will manifest the peace you desire. Begin to feel peaceful, tranquil, and calm as you meditate on these prayers.

Step One: Relax and let go of all tension and anxiety.

Step Two: Tune into your heart center, feeling the peace that this place creates. Feel yourself becoming peaceful.

Step Three: Begin to think only positive thoughts about yourself and your life. You may also include positive thoughts about God, angels, and the universe. The more you concentrate on these thoughts, the more reality will begin to reflect them in your life.

Step Four: Breathe in and out calmly, feeling peace, filling your body with each breath. You may pray for help to achieve a peaceful mind, such as when dealing with the panic and anxiety you may feel when going through changes. Ask Archangel Uriel to help you achieve a peaceful state of mind during these experiences and support you during this time by helping you find positive, helpful, and constructive ways to deal with your anxiety.

Step Five: When you feel relaxed enough, thank the angels for their help and conclude your exercise.

Prayer for Love in Your Life

You can pray for help in finding your true love and happiness. Pray for the strength, courage, and strength to find the qualities of love you seek. Ask Archangel Uriel to help you use your mind to create a deep, abiding sense of love and trust in your life. Pray for extra help and guidance as you work toward this goal. You can use meditation to help you achieve this with the following steps:

Step One: Relax your mind and body. Take a few deep breaths, tune into your body, and relax.

Step Two: Focus on breathing in a way that allows you to relax more each time you inhale and exhale.

Step Three: Imagine love flowing into your heart center. Feel it filling your heart center with love and kindness.

Step Four: Ask the angels to fill your heart center with unconditional love. Ask them to help you feel connected to all people and things around you. Allow the divine light of love to surround you, protecting you against anything that is not conducive to bringing out the best in all people and things.

Step Five: Give thanks for this opportunity to heal and release yourself from this burden of loneliness.

Chapter Ten: Working with Spirit Guides beyond Archangels

In the past, up until recently, most people focused on worshiping gods and goddesses from other cultures. These deities visited people through visions and dreams that priests and shamans interpreted. Most religions overlooked the spiritual power in everyone's hearts and focused on external objects such as statues reminiscent of gods to help people learn about the divine. The issue with this is that many people looking for a spiritual experience found themselves shut out by the traditional limitations of religion and spirituality. Now they turn to less mainstream practices, and with a little guidance, anyone can explore the benefits of spirituality outside the more traditional concepts of angels, gods, and goddesses.

Most people are familiar with angels as heavenly entities who serve as helpers on Earth in various ways, but not everyone is aware that departed loved ones, ancestors, ascended masters, or elementals can also work as spirit guides. Many people find these other types of spirit guides appealing for one reason or another. As with traditional angelic guides, most of these other non-angelic spirit guides are accessible to everyone, and what they have to offer may help you with your spiritual quest. The type of guide you get is based on your own beliefs and practices, but here are some common types of spirit guides that you may contact to get started:

Communicating with Your Ancestors

The ancestors of ancient times were much more in touch with nature and the worlds beyond than we are now. They learned early on to work with spirits of nature and passed that knowledge down through the generations. Today, many people are looking for ways to reconnect with their inner knowledge, and as a way to do so, many of these practitioners turn to their ancestors.

For some, communicating with their ancestors is as easy as talking to a family member who has passed. For others, it is a serious ritual in which the practitioner makes a special connection with his or her ancestors. In this ritual, you can expect to see visions or visit other dimensions with your ancestors as you ask for help and guidance in your life. When you honor your heritage, you acknowledge that you are part of a larger family. By being yourself as a spiritual being and merging with the higher vibrations, you can tap into the infinite wisdom within your ancestors.

Communicating with your ancestors can be as easy or as complex as you let it be. It is best to use the tools of meditation, visualization, and guided imagery to stay connected with those who have passed on. They can also help you interpret people, places, and events around you. Your ancestors are there to support you in your life, but they do not always have all the answers. They are here to help you develop the wisdom and discernment to live the life you want on this plane.

You can set up a special shrine in your home where you can regularly meditate or simply remain in contact with these guides. It is important to remember that ancestral spirits are not guiding you from beyond the grave but rather from the very source of life within you, so they are more than willing to help guide you through the process of learning and self-discovery. When you are ready, you can begin with the following steps:

Step One: Relax into a comfortable position. Take a few deep breaths and clear your mind of all thoughts.

Step Two: Hold one or two of your hands over the area in your chest just below the collar bone. This is the center of your body's energy vortex and will help you feel more connected to the energy around you.

Step Three: Begin meditating on "seeing" or "hearing" your ancestor, just as you would do when doing other spiritual work. You should begin to notice different kinds of subtle energy in the atmosphere. It is important that you take your time and don't force anything.

Step Four: If your ancestor is present, you may feel it immediately. You can ask them to speak, and he or they may answer you with their own voice or project feelings, thoughts, and images.

Step Five: It is normal for them to try and send extrasensory messages to draw you closer as you work together. They will shower you with love and light, but it is important that you set clear boundaries between yourself and the spirit guides with whom you are working.

Step Six: When you feel the session is finished, it is time to let your ancestor go. You can do this by thanking them for their help, then asking them to leave. You can also do this by using a prayer or other words that you find helpful.

Step Seven: As you finish, close your session with a few minutes of silence and meditation.

The Ascended Masters

The ascended masters are living and very active in the spiritual planes, but they may not be as available to you as a traditional spirit guide. Some people seem to have a closer affinity to these masters than others. If you are one of those people, it may be that your body is ready to resonate with these higher vibrations, but each master will still choose who they want to work with.

It is important to remember that the ascended masters are not exactly masters of magic because they are not from this earthly plane. They are spirit guides who choose to move beyond the physical body but still greatly influence this world. Some people call them ascended because they have risen to a higher level of consciousness, but others say that they have transcended from an earthly plane to a higher dimension.

Ascended masters communicate in many ways. Some may speak to you through your mind, others may appear in your dreams, and others may communicate through signs and symbols. Some may appear physically, but this is the rarest and hard-to-get method of communicating with a master. You can also ask questions, and they will answer them telepathically. If you do not hear the voice within your head, it may manifest as an answer to a question you have been pondering in your mind.

To communicate with masters, you may need to have some personal experience working with spirit guides and some training as a psychic medium. If you are not a trained spiritual worker, you may want to listen and allow the master's access to your mind without trying to analyze the communication.

To begin communicating with these masters, you should use a meditative state in which you turn within yourself and reach out beyond the physical world into an astral realm. You may see images in your mind or hear symbols with which you are not familiar. As you travel within yourself, you may find other types of spirit guides that help to translate messages for the ascended masters.

There are different ways in which these guides can communicate with you, and, in the end, it is up to the master to decide how he or she will engage with you. Once you have identified a master guide who resonates with you, it is important to open yourself to them by consciously thinking about them often. Open your mind to the synchronicities in your life that will help you to recognize their presence. A master's frequent visits are often preceded by intuitive feelings, flashes of light, or even strong smells. If a master does visit in physical form, he or she will likely give you a sign that he or she is there. You may feel a discernible pressure on your shoulder blade, experience sudden goosebumps, or see orbs of light appear out of nowhere.

A master's mission is to guide you down the path of light and enlightenment. He or she will help you to align yourself with your Higher Self. The only reason that a master contacts you is because they believe that you have the potential to do great things in the world. Remember that even if no contact is made initially, it does not mean that a master does not feel there is spiritual potential for growth. It is important not to judge the failure of a master to communicate as an indication that they think you are unfit. Many factors are behind why a master chooses one person over another, and it may simply be that they do not feel you would benefit from their help.

A Totem Animal

The role of a spirit animal is to help you connect with your soul's purpose. Your totem is there to guide you on your journey and keep you focused on the path that was chosen for you. It is best if your relationship with an animal begins in childhood but can also happen later in life. Many people believe that spirit animals choose us rather than the other way around. In your childhood, you may not have been aware that a spirit animal could have been trying to communicate with you through dreams and instincts. As you grow up, however, you may begin to hear them in your subconscious, as these guides can send natural signs and omens to help you take the next step on your journey.

To understand how to work with your totem, it is crucial to understand its role within your life. Your spirit animal is there to act as your guide. The animal's presence can help you to understand the meaning behind certain events in your life. It is particularly helpful when you feel confused – or are experiencing mental fogginess. Its presence can also help to clear your mind so that you can concentrate on being present in the moment.

Your totem animal will often help you to access your subconscious mind. When you feel a strong urge to write or think about something, your spirit animal is likely trying to communicate with you. For example, some people feel compelled to write in their journals when they are sitting in traffic or on a bus. These are very common occurrences for those who have spirit animals. If you want to work with an animal guide, you must be aware of these instinctive impulses and follow them up until they yield more information.

Animals can help us learn how to listen and tune into our intuition. They can send us messages that speak directly to our hearts, and there is no doubt that they can be very wise and intuitive friends. As with any animal guide, you should be open to the messages being communicated to you, as it is likely that they will bring guidance and wisdom to your life.

Elemental Spirits

It is easy to forget that we are all part of a vast universe and that even the air we breathe, the water we drink, and the fire we use are alive. The elementals of nature surround us constantly, but most people do not recognize them as beings at all. This can be a problem, as each elemental has a positive purpose to fulfill in your life. Whether your guides are elemental spirits or not, you must learn how to work with Earth energies and elements. Elemental energies are the building blocks of nature and are very powerful, especially when harnessed by a trained practitioner.

Connecting with the elementals is a very different process than working with other types of guides or spirits. They can be easily identified by their energy which is very different from that of your other guides. They are often less organized than spirit guides, so it is best to work with them consciously rather than allowing them to come in and out of your life without your permission. Elemental energies can be unpredictable, so you must learn how to work carefully with them.

There are many ways to identify the elements you may have in your life. One way is to perform divination, such as scrying or dowsing, or to use a pendulum. You can also simply ask the elemental to introduce itself to you by performing a ritual or spell dedicated to the elemental in question.

Elemental spirits communicate in different ways than other spirits do. The most commonly used method of communication is energy dreams. These dreams are very vivid and intense, unlike normal dreams. They are also quite different from lucid dreaming, though some have reported lucid elementals. Some people have also had experiences with elemental personas, which are essentially an element personified into a human form.

Regardless of the method you use to connect with your elementals, you must approach them respectfully and consciously, ensuring that you respect the power they hold in nature and their individual identities and personalities.

Connecting with Your Higher Self

More and more people are learning to connect with their higher selves or the "I" within. This is a term that different religions and spiritual traditions have used to describe the eternal self or soul, the spark of divinity within each of us. There are many ways that you can connect with this part of yourself. The best way is to meditate and clear your mind of all thoughts and anxiety, relaxing into a state of awareness. You can speak directly to your higher self while in this state. You can also use guided meditation, guided imagery, or hypnosis to connect with your higher self.

Once you have established a connection, you must respect and listen to the messages they give you. These messages are often universal truths that help us understand our purpose, goals, and plans for the future. Sometimes they can be difficult to understand, and you may need a spirit guide to help you interpret the message's meaning. Always remember that your higher self is there to help you, protect you, and show you the way. It is your divine source of light, wisdom, love, and power. This energy often works at the highest levels of Creation and helps guide those who are lost along their spiritual path.

It is also important to remember that your higher self exists in a different dimension. Therefore, it cannot be accessed within the physical body. This can be confusing for some people, who may wonder how their higher self communicates with them if it cannot reside within the body. The key is that the communication does not take place on a physical level and therefore cannot be accessed by physical means.

When you first connect with your spirit guides, you may be surprised by the intensity of their energy. This can be overwhelming if you are not already sensitive to this kind of energy. The best way to deal with the energy is to be open and patient. You can also set yourself up for success by respecting all the different kinds of energy that are present and ensuring that you have time and energy to perform the work of connecting and communicating with them.

Some people find that they begin to consciously work with spirit guides right away, while others need to be more open and sensitive to the idea before communicating with guides. It is crucial that you take your time and find what works best for you because it is unlikely that a guide will force themselves on you if you are not ready for them. You can prepare yourself for the work that is to come by meditating with intention, learning how to commune with spirits, and preparing your home for communication and manifestation.

Conclusion

This book has guided what holy books say is true and the evidence supporting these beliefs. It is a great place to start if you are interested in angels and want an understanding of your faith. I hope this will be an opening for anyone looking for guidance, comfort, or just curious about these beings that are said to have watched over us since the beginning of time.

Reaching out to archangels to work with them does not have to be rocket science, nor does it have to be the domain of only the "holy men and women" who have meditated for years, worn the cloth, or know religious texts from cover to cover. It is something you can do as long as you make sure that you are clear in your intentions – *and believe.*

Belief is a very important factor here, and it is the main thing that many scientific studies and minds are missing when they try to look into the phenomenon of archangels and other spiritual and energy beings around us. If you really want to have a transformative experience, you have to be willing to suspend your disbelief. It may be helpful to keep this endeavor to yourself so that no one makes you feel silly for choosing to reach out to a higher power to make your life easier.

Countless others are doing exactly this, and it is why their lives seem touched with otherworldly grace. There is no reason on this little blue dot that you should not have access to the power and might of archangels. So, choose today to take all that you have learned and put in the work. Odds are, your life will never remain the same once you start, and it will change for the better.

Here's another book by Silvia Hill that you might like

Free Bonus from Silvia Hill available for limited time

Hi Spirituality Lovers!

My name is Silvia Hill, and first off, I want to THANK YOU for reading my book.

Now you have a chance to join my exclusive spirituality email list so you can get the ebooks below for free as well as the potential to get more spirituality ebooks for free! Simply click the link below to join.

P.S. Remember that it's 100% free to join the list.

~~$27~~ FREE BONUSES

- 9 Types of Spirit Guides and How to Connect to Them
- How to Develop Your Intuition: 7 Secrets for Psychic Development and Tarot Reading
- Tarot Reading Secrets for Love, Career, and General Messages

Access your free bonuses here
https://livetolearn.lpages.co/spirit-guides-and-archangels-paperback/

References

Andrews, T. (1992). How to meet & work with spirit guides. Llewellyn Worldwide.

Blumenthal, S. (1990). Spotted Cattle and Deer: Spirit Guides and Symbols of Endurance and Healing in" Ceremony. "American Indian Quarterly.

Ching, E. D., & Ching, K. (2006). Faces of your soul: Rituals in art, mask making, and guided imagery with ancestors, spirit guides, and totem animals. North Atlantic Books.

Farmer, S. D. (2012). Pocket Guide to Spirit Animals: Understanding Messages from Your Animal Spirit Guides. Hay House, Inc.

Dominguez, I. (2008). Spirit Speak: Knowing and Understanding Spirit Guides, Ancestors, Ghosts, Angels, and the Divine. Red Wheel/Weiser.

Elder, P. (2005). Eyes of an Angel: Soul Travel, Spirit Guides, Soul Mates, and the Reality of Love. Hampton Roads Publishing.

Farmer, S. D. (2006). Animal Spirit Guides: An easy-to-use handbook for identifying and understanding your power animals and animal spirit helpers. Hay House, Inc.

Farmer, S. D. (2012). Pocket Guide to Spirit Animals: Understanding Messages from Your Animal Spirit Guides. Hay House, Inc.

Fisher, J. (2001). The Siren Call of Hungry Ghosts: A Riveting Investigation into Channeling and Spirit Guides. Cosimo, Inc.

Goodare, J. (2020). Emotional relationships with spirit guides in early modern Scotland. In The supernatural in early modern Scotland (pp. 39-54). Manchester University Press.

Jacobs, C. F. (1989). Spirit guides and possession in the New Orleans black spiritual churches. Journal of American folklore.

Marciniak, B. (1992). Bringers of the Dawn: Teachings from the Pleiadians. Simon and Schuster.

Porter, J. E. (1996). Spiritualists, Aliens, and UFOs: Extraterrestrials as spirit guides. Journal of Contemporary Religion.

Webster, R. (1998). Spirit Guides & Angel Guardians: Contact Your Invisible Helpers. Llewellyn Worldwide.

Berner, C. (2007). The Four (or Seven) Archangels in the First Book of Enoch and Early Jewish Writings of the Second Temple Period. Deuterocanonical and Cognate Literature Yearbook, 2007.

Cline, R. H. (2011). Archangels, Magical Amulets, and the Defense of Late Antique Miletus. Journal of Late Antiquity, 4.

Dix, G. H. (1927). The Seven Archangels and the Seven Spirits: A Study in the Origin, Development, and Messianic Associations of the Two Themes. The Journal of Theological Studies, 28.

Green, M. (2010). The Four Archangels: Angelic Inspiration for a Balanced, Joyous Life. Xlibris Corporation.

Jameson, A. B. (1857). Sacred and Legendary Art: Containing Legends of the Angels and Archangels, the Evangelists, the Apostles, the Doctors of the Church, and St. Mary Magdalene, as Represented in the Fine Arts (Vol. 1). Longmans, Green, and Company.

Łaptaś, M. (2016). Archangel Raphael as protector, demon tamer, guide, and healer. Some aspects of the Archangel's activities in Nubian painting. In Aegyptus et Nubia Christiana. The Włodzimierz Godlewski jubilee volume on the occasion of his 70th birthday (pp. 459-479). Wydawnictwa Uniwersytetu Warszawskiego.

Sandu, I., Iurcovschi, C. T., Sandu, I. G., Vasilache, V., Negru, I. C., Brebu, M., ... & Pelin, V. A. S. I. L. E. (2019). Multianalytical Study for Establishing the Historical Contexts of the Church of the Holy Archangels from Cicau, Alba County, Romania, for its Promotion as a World Heritage Good I. Assessing the preservation-restoration works from the 18th century. Revista de Chimie.

Virtue, D. (2010). Archangels and Ascended Masters. ReadHowYouWant. com.

Virtue, D. (2011). Archangels 101: How to Connect Closely with Archangels Michael, Raphael, Gabriel, Uriel, and Others for Healing, Protection, and Guidance. Hay House Incorporated